I AM
THE SECRET
FOOTBALLER

I AM THE SECRET FOOTBALLER

Lifting the Lid on
the Beautiful Game

guardianbooks

Published by Guardian Books 2012

2 4 6 8 10 9 7 5 3 1

First published in Great Britain in 2012 by
Guardian Books
Kings Place, 90 York Way
London N1 9GU

www.guardianbooks.co.uk

A CIP catalogue record for this book is
available from the British Library

ISBN 978 0852 65308 1

Text design by seagulls.net
Cover design by Mark Ecob

Printed and bound by CPI Group (UK) Ltd, Croydon, CR0 4YY

Mixed Sources
Product group from well-managed
forests and other controlled sources
www.fsc.org Cert no. TT-COC-2139
© 1996 Forest Stewardship Council

Guardian Books supports The Forest Stewardship Council (FSC),
the leading international forest certification organisation. All our titles that
are printed on Greenpeace approved FSC certified paper carry the FSC logo.

CONTENTS

INTRODUCTION

Paul Johnson, Deputy Editor, Guardian News and Media

"I am The Secret Footballer" is both a declaration and a device. Since he wrote his first column for the Guardian 18 months ago, there has been a sustained effort to unmask The Secret Footballer. Jigsaw identification has been attempted through forensic analysis of his pieces using names, games, clubs and matches. Fans' forums debate in a knowledgeable and thoughtful way. There is a dedicated website at whoisthesecretfootballer.co.uk. Dozens of players have been identified as him. According to those who think they have cracked a code, he plays for Blackburn, Sunderland, Fulham, Bolton, Wolves, Burnley, Newcastle, Leicester, Liverpool, West Ham, Everton, Spurs, Birmingham or Celtic. And a few others.

On his Wikipedia page the entry says he is English and has turned out for at least two Premier League clubs. The argument and search for clues are fun and understandable – and it may be that some day he will decide to reveal himself as the author. But to write as he does, in such detail about the game and the people in it, would be impossible out in the open. His club(s) wouldn't like it, and would probably cite breach of contract. His agent wouldn't like it and his manager(s) would be somewhere on the other side of incandescent.

He tells us what it is like to score against Manchester United; about John Terry and his own reaction to being whacked in the face with an elbow: "I kicked him as hard as I could across the back of the legs and he crumpled to the ground." He describes vividly the impact on life of a £1.4m-a-year contract (along with a £19,000-a-month mortgage) and how, in his words, it "opens up a host of recreational possibilities". The sharks, the brown envelopes, the deals, the convoluted bonuses; malicious managers and understanding managers; supportive team-mates and those tortured and fearful of the end; the media, the women and the drink are all here, in a range that goes from the amusing to the terrifying.

But The Secret Footballer is different, and those differences which mark him out started early on in life. He describes his working-class background, playing in hand-me-down trainers. He came out of a loving and supportive family with his father encouraging him to read classics – Shakespeare, Dickens, Joyce etc. He didn't get into football by the usual route and has struggled with the paradox of living a dream playing football but having to deal with the aggravations and frustrations off the pitch. The same tension shows with his continued determination not to leave his roots behind while developing a taste for fine wine, art and luxurious holidays. Those pressures built up to the point where he became insecure, reclusive and volatile; seeking help and put on medication after finding himself coming home from training and sitting in the same chair until it was time for bed. All of it is told as the reality of his life.

Some years ago, reading the FT at weekends, The Secret Footballer enjoyed a column written anonymously by an estate agent which opened up a world many buyers and sellers have extensive experience of, but which, to those in the know, is very different: far more complex, potentially dangerous and duplicitous. The comparisons with football were only too obvious. Football, a game watched by millions, is digested and dissected in fine detail in print, on the radio, on TV and on the web. Managers and players give interviews, ex-pros write columns. Tactics, personalities, money and motives are debated endlessly. And yet what do we really understand? The Secret Footballer's answer to that is simple: not that much.

So he had the idea for a column. We (Ian Prior, the Guardian's sports editor and myself) were approached and thought it had amazing potential. But we were worried: would he write honestly, what would he hold back, could he sustain themes, could he write at all? All those thoughts disappeared the moment the first piece arrived – and he has got better and better ever since. This book was his idea. It is all his own words, his own experiences, his own thoughts, his own emotions. He is a remarkable man.

Paul Johnson

London, August 2012

CHAPTER 1
FIRST STEPS

When I started playing football for a living, I vowed that I would never turn out like the embittered older professionals that my new club seemed to have made a point of collecting. Far from offering any advice or guidance, they took every opportunity to rub my face in a mistake or faux pas. In those days I had no idea that footballers started training at 10am and finished at midday. I remember hanging around in the changing room after my first session waiting to be told that I could go home. Nobody sits you down with a "how to" guidebook and fills you in on football etiquette. You're either what managers refer to as "streetwise", or you're too naive for your own good. In my case, I was as raw as my football.

I still think that I am incredibly lucky never to have gone through the youth system, for two reasons. Firstly, I have always had huge problems with anyone in authority, especially if that authority is abused for the purpose of making the rulemaker feel more important than they actually are. Secondly, I much prefer to play what has become known as "street football". You can spot a manufactured footballer a mile off but the players who are naturally gifted and are almost uncoachable nearly always offer the most excitement. For example, Lionel Messi and Wayne Rooney do not need to be coached: they play like they did in the street as 10-year-olds. Granted, they may need integrating into a style of play or formation but on the whole they are playing off the cuff. I am no Messi or Rooney – let's make that absolutely clear – but for the best part of my career I played as if I had nothing to lose. I loved going up against players who had been given everything on a plate, and walking off to collect a bottle of champagne for man of the match. Not because I like champagne – it just felt like a victory for all the people back home who never made it to the big time.

As a newcomer, I immediately made a beeline for the corner of the dressing room, far enough away from the dominant players and close enough to keep my face in the manager's eyeline. Unfortunately, on my first day as a professional, a Scandinavian player, who was one of the embittered old pros, took exception to my choice of seat and threw my clothes all over the changing room while I was having lunch. I came back to find my belongings strewn over the corridor and in the shower room. This was a shock for me: I'd assumed that a team was exactly that – a team, a group of people who looked out for each other, helped each other and fought as one. How wrong I was. If there is one thing that I have learned, it is that every single player in every single dressing room has an agenda. It doesn't matter if they are your closest friend or your sworn enemy – everyone is in it for themselves. The realisation that some of these players were playing football because it paid the bills and, worse, that many of them were terrible, was an eye-opener for me. But at the same time it gave me the most enormous confidence boost.

As a kid I played football day and night – I used to take a football to bed with me so that I could do keep-ups as soon as I woke up, before school. Every day after it I'd go through the VHS version of 101 Great Goals (the one with Bobby Charlton on the cover), crossing off each goal as I recreated it either in the park, with the swings wrapped behind the metal posts, or "down the back", where there were two perfectly proportioned chestnut trees that provided more space to pull off the long shots like Emlyn Hughes's screamer for Liverpool (I can't remember the number now but it was a personal favourite because you could hear Hughes yelling wildly as he celebrated the goal).

That's why I wanted to play football: it held the possibility of so much glory and happiness and an escape from the mundane life that came with growing up in a small town. My ambition was to win the World Cup. I had a 1986 Panini sticker album that my dad bought for me, and looking at all the foreign players in their different-coloured strips was so exciting – players like Socrates and Russia's Rats, Rummenigge and, of course, Maradona. It offered a doorway to the wider world and I was hooked. Years later one of my team-mates was called up to play for England; he was the first player I knew to be selected for the squad. It was an exciting time for everybody and I couldn't wait to ask him what it was like. "Oh, it's quality, mate," he told me. "They give you 50 grand just for your image rights."

I can't tell you how happy playing football made me as a kid. It was just the best thing in the world to be able to go outside and kick a ball around for hours pretending to be Ian Rush or Glenn Hoddle. But although I was immersed in football, my dad took it upon himself to educate me, and not only in the game he loved. The small group of people who know I'm the Secret Footballer have all asked me the same question: where do the bizarre, and sometimes leftfield, hooks to the column come from? The answer is Dad's vast collection of literary classics, including Shakespeare, Dickens and Joyce, and original vinyl from greats such as the Beatles, Pink Floyd, Dylan, the Stones etc. While some of my friends went for the traditional beach holiday, Dad would think nothing of driving to Denmark for two weeks on a farm, listening to drug-inspired rock'n'roll while we were made to read literary classics in the back seat. For a 10-year-old, I'd argue that's not normal. But I wouldn't change it for the world.

Not that I was an academic. I found one of my old school reports that reads, "****** does not listen and so misses key instructions, leading to his falling behind." The subsequent improvement in my attention only highlighted a startling inability to care about what was being said. Football was all I wanted to do: it was morning, noon and night and I was convinced I'd "make it". My parents encouraged my football career and every weekend drove me to my next match. I played for the best local teams, the county and district sides, as well as my school, and was known in our area as one of a crop of very talented players who were emerging. Some of these players did go on to become professionals, some drifted into respectable jobs, and others, like me, didn't have a clue what to do if a football career never materialised. And as the years went by the prospect of playing profes-sional football began to seem as likely as my getting any further up Kate Brookes' inside leg during our science lessons.

Around the age of 15 and 16, a few of my team-mates were picked up by professional clubs, the pinnacle of which was when a lad signed for Tottenham's academy (he was released two years later). I had trials myself and generally performed well but my situation wasn't helped by the fact that scouts in this country are not coaches or managers.

Whenever I went along to one of these trials, the lads who were 4ft nothing would immediately be put out on the wing to rot, while the ones who were a foot taller than everyone else were put in at centre-back, despite telling their scout that they were a centre midfielder or a target man. Time and again this happened. It used to piss me off but, more than that, it used to piss off my dad, who'd had to drive to the end of the country to see his son played as a right-back for an hour and then at left wing for 15 minutes.

In fairness, scouting for kids at the top hasn't improved that much. At the very top of the game, the trawler net has never been bigger and it has never been easier to land a prize catch. A friend of mine who has been a scout for a leading club for more than 10 years told me that if he were lazy, he'd never even have to leave his office because clubs further down the footballing pyramid regularly call him up to offer their best youngsters. "Every year those phone calls come a little earlier and the kids get younger." And he should know.

In early 2012, Chelsea paid £1.5m for Patrick Bamford, an 18-year-old striker who had played only 12 minutes of first-team football for Nottingham Forest. Frank Clark, the Forest chairman, explained how things have changed. "We used to be able to hold on to players for a couple of years into the first team, but now the real big clubs are paying fortunes for kids of 13, 14, 15, 16." The scary thing is that my friend admits he doesn't even have to get it right. "If I beat off the competition from the other big teams I've done my job. If the player doesn't become a first-team regular, then that's the coach's fault, not mine."

When bigger names are involved, it is easier still. A few years ago I was talking to another friend of mine who at the time was the chief scout for one of the top clubs in the Premier League. We were having coffee and I casually asked how life was. His team had just won the Premier League title and I expected it to be all sunshine and happiness. But his answer caught me completely off guard. "Every year it's the same, mate. After the manager and the coaching staff get the budget through from the owners, we all sit down to run through the possible transfer targets. They'll look at me and say: 'We need an attacking midfielder.' And I'll say: 'OK, well, there's Totti, Kaka and Ronaldinho.'" I have no experience as a chief scout but, if the day ever comes when I'm offered this position at a top club, I can't see it being overly demanding.

In terms of my own attempts to break through, it was pretty hard seeing some of my team-mates picked up by professional clubs. I didn't feel they were as skilful as me – stronger maybe, and certainly better-built at the age of 15, but definitely not as good with the ball. Unfortunately, at that time clubs were more interested in physical attributes than in technical ability.

Thankfully, while a lot of my friends were "experimenting" in the drugs scene of the late 1990s, I'd managed, mentally at least, to escape. I had made the decision that whatever I was going to do in my life, a good proportion of it would not be spent wasting away in my home town, where precious little of any interest ever happened. It was while I was planning my getaway (a week before I was due to leave the country) that my mum took a telephone call from a scout asking if her son would like to come for a trial match next week with a team he was working for. At the time, I was playing non-league and picking up about £30 per week. As I later found out, the scout had been contacted by one of my old managers, who had told him that I had enough potential to warrant a second look, provided the club felt it could commit to enough extra coaching to turn me into a polished professional.

I don't remember an awful lot about that trial match. My head was still filled with the possibility of what I was starting to think of as freedom, so at half time when the manager collared me in the tunnel and said, "Cancel your holidays – we're going to sign you," any joy that I may have felt was tempered by the fact that I had paid for a one-way ticket to San Francisco and was only really thinking about what I still had to buy from Superdrug.

I have thought about that moment almost every day since. I wonder what would have happened if I'd had the strength to turn him down. Despite wanting to play professional football since I could walk, I had seen enough of life to realise that once you are tied into something, it is often very difficult to get your liberty back. I wonder where I'd be now. Would I have won medals and enjoyed 15 minutes of fame and recognition for doing something well? Would I have had those intense moments of sheer happiness after scoring a goal or winning a crucial match? The real questions to ask are: would I have more "real friends" if I'd been around for just one weekend in the last dozen years? Would I have been able to make my best friend's wedding, where I was supposed to be best man, rather than getting turned over at Arsenal? Would I have been able to attend the funerals that I have missed, and where my absences have mostly never been forgiven? Would I be on anti-depressants, as I am now? Would I have pissed off the amount of people I have because I just don't want to be like them? And would I know how to measure my life in real terms, rather than by money and success on a football pitch? Again, who knows? As somebody once said, football was my favourite game.

But I did sign (£500 a week, which was a fortune to me) and I set about my new-found career with the overriding feeling that they'd let someone in the door that perhaps they shouldn't have, an outsider into the inner sanctum. And now that I was in, there was fuck-all anybody could do about it. That feeling has never left me.

If I'm honest, my first impressions were that I'd made a massive mistake. The standard was poor, some of the players were detestable and the lifestyle was something that was completely alien to me. I'd sit at home for hours in the afternoons wondering what to do, and when I came into train the next day I'd get abuse for being "different", whatever that means. Because I had no experience of player "banter", some of the more vocal members of the squad would hammer me every day for their own amusement. Pastimes included saying "Shhh" every time I tried to speak until eventually I'd have to give up, or trying to get me to remove my hat when we had lunch, claiming it breached club rules. Then there was the time they stole my phone and texted the manager, thanking him for "last night".

I remember one day sitting in the changing room before training, when some of the senior pros were talking about a "third man run". Having never heard this term, I innocently asked if they could explain it to me. They just looked at me in utter disgust. The silence was only broken when one of the more bitter players, who wasn't getting a game at that point, said: "And we wonder why we don't win many games when we're signing this sort of shit."

There were other incidents that stick in my mind. A few of the senior players would pass the ball at me as hard as they could in a weak attempt to make me miscontrol it, which was pathetic, although I've since found out this sort of initiation test happens at every level. On Dwight Yorke's first day as a Manchester United player, Roy Keane fired the ball into him deliberately hard so the striker would be unable to handle it. "Welcome to United," Keane said. "Cantona used to kill them." As much as I resented what the senior players were doing to me, in some ways it worked because I always arrived at training before anybody else, and left last. It strengthened my desire to be better than them and leave them behind.

After about six months, I had demonstrated that I was more than capable of playing at this level. I was performing consistently and regularly winning the man-of-the-match award (we couldn't afford champagne, so it was just a photograph with the sponsor and an acknowledgment in the next home programme). I was beginning to make a name for myself, which meant that those who had made life difficult for me initially began to ease off. Around this time, the manager was able to move a good number of the older players on and my standing in the changing room went from zero to hero. I had certainly come a long way from my debut, when I remember hearing one of the away fans call out my surname. Stupidly, I thought that somebody I knew from back home had come to watch me, so I turned to look. With that, the whole stand shouted "Waaaaanker!" before laughing uncontrollably. I'd completely forgotten that playing football at this level meant you had your name plastered on the back of your shirt.

I still didn't particularly like the day-to-day life of a footballer. I enjoyed the games, even though we were by no means world-beaters, but during the week there was absolutely nothing to do apart from sit at home and read or watch TV. Often I'd try to stay at the club for as long as possible just for something to do. I'd spend hours hitting the ball against a wall that had numbered squares on it. Sometimes we'd play against each other – you had to hit all six squares in order and the first to do it won a fiver. But there was only so much you could do at the club on any given day. The facilities were fairly basic: we had a head-tennis court that was a death trap as it was surrounded by razor-wire, and a car park that doubled as a space to practise long passing until I smashed the manager's window and ruined it for everyone. My long passing has since improved but the £180 bill for a single pane of glass still strikes me as steep.

On a normal day we would meet at the stadium before travelling to the training ground. I didn't have a car so I would grab a ride with a player who sat next to me in the changing room along with his circle of friends. They were a very tight group of black players and I'd have to put up with some pretty awful R&B on the ride over, but for some reason they warmed to me and christened me an "honorary brother". The title meant that they had my back; if I was in trouble, they would look after me, and if I made a mistake, they would tell me. And when it came to the point when I was on the verge of leaving the club for pastures new, they made phone calls to some of their old clubs on my behalf. I owe them a lot for their grounding.

The difference between bullying and banter is best illustrated by something that this group of players used to do. Once a week, one of them would come in early and set up a sort of makeshift barber shop. Then, one by one, the other black players would come in and have their hair clipped and styled while reading magazines. I was always the first player to arrive from outside this group and felt that they had warmed to me sufficiently for me to start engaging in banter of my own. So I would say: "Fuck me, Desmond's here again." Or I'd nick the scissors and pretend to cut the hair of whoever was sat in the chair, while playing the barber from the movie Coming to America. "Every time I start talking about boxing, a white man gotta pull Rocky Marciano out they ass. Fuck you, fuck you and fuck you. Who's next?" I think they laughed out of pity, as my impressions were average at best, but it was great for race relations. One day, however, I walked through the door and was jumped by five black men wielding a set of clippers, who then set about shaving off all my hair. And I do mean *all* my hair.

As I became better known, I began to taste the benefits that came with being a professional footballer. By this time, I'd left home and moved closer to the ground and was living near another player who I travelled in with. As our club had next to no money, we'd have to travel to away matches on the day of the game, which is unheard of higher up in football. We'd arrive back late, sometimes 2am or 3am, depending on where we'd been playing, before getting in the car and driving the 20 miles or so back home. At that hour the streets are almost empty and we'd generally go through red lights and get up to a fair speed as we made our way out of the city. One day, however, we were pulled over by a policeman on a motorbike and, fearing the worst, we got our excuses ready. In the event we needn't have bothered. As soon as the officer saw the pair of us in our club tracksuits, he began to congratulate us on the result of the game before escorting us out of the city.

From that moment on we had a police escort to the nearest A-road after almost every away game. He would wait for us to arrive back at the stadium and have a quick chat about the result, the club and football in general before seeing us safely out of town. I suppose that would be the highlight of the graveyard shift for a policeman in that part of the world, and we were certainly grateful. I do remember that we used to beat ourselves up about whether we should give him something for his help besides the kebab we always offered when we'd stop for some late dinner. We eventually decided on a club pin-badge (money was tight back then) and to our delight he wore it on his police jacket for the rest of our time at the club. And he probably still does.

Thinking back to those days, though, there are many reasons why being a virtual nobody made playing football so much more enjoyable. There was little pressure on the club or me to do well but I was very hungry to succeed anyway; that is a fantastic combination, and something I'd give a lot to experience again. The manager expected me to make mistakes, as did the fans, but I always wanted to be perfect, and so long as my performances fell somewhere in the middle I knew I was doing OK. Very often, though, they were excellent and pretty soon I became a big fish in a small pond.

To see this same situation played out today, with me being the elder statesman, does not make me unhappy, or bitter, or jealous. Instead, I try to help where I can to improve the next generation of players, even if sometimes it is incredibly frustrating when they can't do something that senior players take for granted.

A few years ago, I gave serious consideration to giving up football altogether to pursue my other passions, only to have a moment of clarity that prompted a complete rethink. Sometimes when the games are coming thick and fast, and you don't see your family, you aren't playing wonderfully well and the results are poor, things can get on top of you. I would later come to realise that this was depression knocking at the door, and my answer to it was that I'd be much happier doing something else. Standing in the tunnel before a match against Liverpool at Anfield, I had a brush with something that Marcel Proust describes as "a remembrance of things past". As our coach gave each player a ball, I lifted mine up to my nose and sniffed it. Don't ask me why – I had never done it before as a professional, or since. The ball was brand new and looked so inviting. The smell took me right back to my council estate and the moment when my mum and dad bought me one of my first full-size footballs, an Adidas Tango. Everybody knows that smell of a new football and at that moment it suddenly filled me with all the reasons I had ever wanted to play the game – it smelled of happy times and familiarity. As the noise outside grew louder and the familiar opening notes of You'll Never Walk Alone made their way through the tunnel, I told myself to keep that moment at the front of my mind for as long as possible.

It is often said that 95% of what happens in football takes place behind closed doors and, believe me, the truth is far stranger than fiction. You might see us for 90 minutes on a Saturday and form many of your opinions about football purely on that fleeting appearance. You might watch analysts drone on about tactics without realising what they are saying is predesigned to fit a narrative and barely scratches the surface. Perhaps you've read about the infamous Christmas parties in the tabloids and wonder if they are as crazy as they would have you believe. Maybe you simply don't understand how young, seemingly healthy athletes, who appear to have it all, can be depressed. Maybe you have seen a couple of the so-called Wags on TV and wonder what their lives are really like. Perhaps you've always wondered how a player can perform poorly for one club and yet blossom at another. Is there really a racist undercurrent in the modern game? How important is the manager or the captain? Are the officials biased towards the big teams? What do players really think of TV pundits, the FA and Fifa? What are the benefits of the foreign players or a top agent on transfer deadline day? How do player bonuses work? What matters more, cash or cups? And what do players really think of you, the fans?

The only way you would ever find out the answers to many of those questions is to read a book that was written in total anonymity by a player who has played at the highest level. In this book, I will try to explain exactly how football really works, away from the prying eyes of the outside world, by drawing on my own experiences. Many of these stories I shouldn't be telling you about. But I will.

CHAPTER 2
MANAGERS

What makes a good manager? I've played for great managers, and I've also played for one or two who were so bad that I would happily have faked my own death to get out of working with them for a minute longer. The best managers gain the absolute trust of their players, put you on your toes whenever they set foot in the room, and have a playing philosophy that is greeted with enthusiasm and carried on to the pitch with spirit and belief. Above all, though, a manager must have the respect of everybody at the football club.

Simple qualities are priceless. Players want a manager to be consistent and honest. Nobody wants to sit on the sidelines watching, but an explanation of why you are not in the team, especially if you have only just been dropped, can go a long way to quelling discontent. Players will respect the manager for pulling them aside even if they don't agree with the decision. Man-management skills like this send out signals to the players; they keep everybody united and, as a result, extract the absolute best from a squad. When the opposite happens, unrest festers and stories start to surface about how the manager has "lost the dressing room". This does actually happen – perhaps not as regularly as some would have us believe, but there are certainly occasions when players collectively lose respect for a manager. I've experienced it. At that time, it was because of a shared belief that our tactics were flawed, and that this was making us look like poor players and, in turn, lose matches. Although a manager can sometimes be a convenient scapegoat, on this occasion our unhappiness was completely justified.

Players are subject to disciplinary procedures, but there is no written warning or fine system for managers. Instead players stop trying in training and in matches and lose heart. A friend of mine recently told me that things got so bad at his club that a group of players began to speculate that it was a deliberate ploy by the manager to get himself sacked. After all, where else, apart from maybe in the banking world, can you get a multimillion-pound payoff for failure? This certainly got me thinking about who might have done the same thing.

Managers don't have to be loved. I know a few players who despise their boss but remain extremely successful under him. Similarly, I know one or two managers who put up with a lot of nonsense from some of their players because they are extremely important to the team. It's about mutual respect, not mutual affection.

Some players want to be managers. But some managers still want to be players. I remember at one club being fined for going out to a pub with a couple of friends while injured. Although this was a Tuesday evening, and therefore I had not broken the rule that you must not be on licensed premises 48 hours before a game, my manager claimed that any alcohol would hamper my rehab. He fined me two weeks' wages. I didn't argue, but as I left his room he turned from manager to player and, with a big, fat, stupid grin on his face, said: "By the way, did you get hold of anything?" He was asking if I had escorted a young lady home, although he knew I had a long-term girlfriend. He turned out to be more disappointed that I had no story to tell than with what he was fining me for in the first place. That day we both lost respect for each other but for very different reasons.

I am often asked about fines. Some people seem to have a preoccupation with the money that footballers earn, and I suppose fines are part of that. I can't remember exactly how many times the various clubs that I have represented have officially fined me, but it's no more than half a dozen. As for the times I have had to cough up a fine that goes into the players' pool and contributes to things like a Christmas party or an end-of-season jolly, these must number in the hundreds.

The smaller fines that go into the players' pot range from about £10 to £200 and can be for anything from leaving a water bottle or a piece of kit on the training ground (they both have your squad number on them) to being late for training. But it's not uncommon for a supertax of up to £2,000 to be levied at a top club for a particular misdemeanour – it all depends what crime the players want to attach the fine to. At one club I played for, we had a team-mate who was always late for training, so we put our own £500 supertax on the offence. He still turned up late and, as a result, made a major contribution to the hiring of a private jet for the lads' Christmas party. You may think the fine quite steep for the offence but lateness is, in my view and that of many other players, unnecessary and disrespectful to everyone else.

For a long time, I refused to pay any fines at all. I just couldn't understand how anybody could take money from me unless it was stipulated in a legal and binding contract. At one club we abolished them for a time, much to my delight, but what began to happen was a breakdown in social standards. Many of the players started to take the mickey by arriving late and becoming lazy in their etiquette, deliberately leaving their kit on the training pitch for others to tidy away and parking wherever they wanted. They didn't even turn up for team-bonding piss-ups, which, believe it or not, can be important when it comes to integrating new faces. After a while I began to wish we could fine a few of them to teach them a lesson. The system does seem to work.

The big official fines are quite rare and only come about if there is a complete and obvious breach of the club rules. I know a couple of players who have been fined a week's wages for not turning up to the annual Christmas visit of the children's ward at the local hospital. Sadly, they were happy to pay if it meant not having to go.

I remember when I signed for a new club and couldn't find the spa that they had gone to for the day (no Sat Nav back then). I just went home. The next day the manager asked me what I thought the fine should be. "Probably the day that I missed is fair, gaffer," I said. (Well, it was worth a go.) "Nice try," he said. "If you can't at least be fair about it, then you can give me five days' money instead." That was a lesson learned and about £12,000 lost.

The most unjust fine of all time (and this is my opinion, as there isn't an official list or anything) came a few years back when a manager and I were having a total relationship breakdown and were barely on speaking terms. As a result, he was trying to fine me for the smallest of indiscretions, which is standard practice when trying to get a player out the door. When a player reaches this point at a club it is not uncommon for him to start playing silly buggers by throwing a few sick days in here and there, but on this occasion I was genuinely ill and needed to be near a toilet at all times. I had been awake all night feeling terrible and in the morning I called the physio to tell him I wouldn't be in for training. Five minutes later, having relayed our conversation to the manager, the physio rang me back: "Sorry, mate – he wants you in to see the club doctor." The doc later told me that the manager had actually called him away from his practice in the hope that I wouldn't turn up and then he could fine me for wasting the doc's time and faking illness. "I can't come in," I said. "I've got the shits – I'll never be able to do half an hour in the car." The physio duly told the manager but it didn't cut any ice and I was told that unless I turned up at 10am to see the doc, the manager was going to fine me a week's wages. Only in football can an employee be threatened with a fine for being ill.

I dragged myself to the car, packing extra pants and a towel to sit on (well, there was no need to ruin the leather) and began the drive in. Ten minutes in, I made the first of four stops by the side of the motorway, much to the amusement of the commuters, before arriving at the training ground at 10.40am.

I walked into the training ground and made my way to the physio room. "Bloody hell, you look like shit," he said as I stumbled in and fell on to one of the massage beds. The doc came over, took one look at me, prodded around my stomach for a while and then diagnosed me with gastro-something-or-other. Just then the manager poked his head in the door. "Is he ill?" he said, looking expectantly at the doc. "Yes, gaffer, he most definitely is ill," replied the doc. "Right," said the manager, and turning to me he continued: "You better get yourself back home to bed then, rather than spreading that around here. Oh, and by the way you're fined a grand for being late this morning." I didn't say anything.

I was still fairly young back then, but as you get older and become a more senior member of the squad, things start to change. A manager may ask your opinion from time to time and, since assuming this position, I've found it a challenge to tell the manager what I really think.

During the hiring process for a new manager at one of my clubs, the hierarchy asked me into a room to discuss potential candidates. This is highly unusual and, as I told them at the time, very uncomfortable for a player. Imagine sitting in a room with a board of executives and being asked to "give a view" on potential new bosses: it can only end in disaster. I felt that anything I said was at some stage likely to get back to the new manager as well as the other candidates. So even the managers I knew I wouldn't enjoy working with ended up receiving a glowing review.

The reality is that the last thing a new manager needs is for his players to be calling the shots because that is the slippery slope to ruin. By the same token, he doesn't want to alienate the squad before he gets his feet under the table. The first week of a new manager's reign is often fairly low-key. There are handshakes and pleasantries while he takes in training from afar, making mental notes about each player's game and behaviour.

One or two players will go out of their way to kiss his arse but even as I get older and more aware that this man hands out the contracts, I refuse to break my moral tradition. I do, however, take the time to have a chat about football with him while dropping in little-known names and results from abroad in a fairly weak attempt to showcase my broad knowledge of the game, because I have more than one eye on a part-time scouting-cum-coach role when my playing days are over.

There can be an immediate turnaround in fortunes for a club that changes its manager. I won't say that tactics have nothing to do with it but when I hear a pundit say something like, "He's got them organised", in reference to a team's improved results, I cringe. Often it has little to do with hours spent on the training pitch and more to do with the players trying that much harder.

The indifferent form a team has shown previously can sometimes be put down to the fact that the players have become so comfortable with the manager that they ease off mentally and physically. You'll know this has happened when you hear a manager say: "I have taken this team as far as it can go." That roughly translates to: "This group of players no longer fear or respect me and, ultimately, are no longer motivated by me."

The biggest mistake a new manager can make is to get too close to the players as a way of getting them onside. I had one manager who would crack jokes with us as we were walking out to play a match, only to bollock us for being a goal down at half time. It smacked of double standards and because of that he never had the respect that a manager needs from players earning big wages and harbouring even bigger egos. There are better ways to endear yourself to the players.

A new manager needs to stamp his authority on the squad quickly, and to achieve this very often he will sacrifice a player, as was the case at one of my clubs. It doesn't matter if that player is capable and well liked (actually, these players are the preferred targets). The process generally involves the player being singled out for ridicule in training and made an example of at every opportunity, before being sent to train with the kids and ostracised from the first team. It is meant as a clear message to everyone that the manager is in charge.

I don't like this method: it is completely unnecessary and suggests a total lack of man-management skills. A friend of mine suffered this treatment during the 2011-12 season and, believe me, he wasn't a lot of fun to speak to at the time.

The rise of managers such as Arsène Wenger, José Mourinho, André Villas-Boas and Brendan Rodgers has also won over the players who once believed that the only manager worth signing for was the one who had a few medals tucked away from his playing days. In truth, lots of managers have no input during training and there are more than a few who leave everything to their coaches, especially if they are well liked and respected by the players. I am told that one ex-Manchester United player turned manager has a reputation for showing his face only on Saturday for the game.

Not so long ago I bumped into an acquaintance on a beach in the Caribbean (he was there for an old pros' tournament, which essentially is an old boys' piss-up in the sun courtesy of a sponsor who wants to meet all his heroes) and he invited me for a drink in the hotel bar that evening. I went along not realising that he was going to "open up" to me about how management was not at all like he expected it to be. This man had been looking forward to becoming a manager for years, since his playing career hadn't exactly set the world alight. He loved football and was convinced that he had more than enough to offer if he ever got a chance in the hot seat. He had collected every coaching badge available, including the pro licence that costs about £5,000.

He'd been in his first managerial job for less than a year when he realised he'd made a mistake. "I didn't appreciate just how much there is to do," he told me. "I knew it would be tough and that I would see less of my family, but in the end I wasn't seeing them at all because at 10pm, after I'd finally got off the phone, I would sit in a dark room watching Elfsborg v Malmö in the hope of finding a player."

Being a manager is exactly what it says on the tin. It's about managing situations and problems, whether that's people, tasks, the media, expectations or whatever. When I put it to him that perhaps he had a bit of a problem with the art of delegation (well, if they're down you may as well stick the boot in – that's what I was always taught), he conceded that it could well be a valid criticism. But he also reminded me that I had never been a manager.

I take his point, because I may easily suffer from the same flaw should I ever enter into management. I find it very hard to trust other people with important responsibilities, because invariably they won't do what I would have done with the same task. They will put their own spin on something instead. And if you prefer to retain control of every single decision at a football club, then I'm afraid you won't see your family. You probably won't even see daylight.

I have had a manager like that – a complete control freak who had all the staff a manager could ever need but simply couldn't bring himself to let them get on with their jobs. And these were talented guys. I felt particularly sorry for our sports scientist, who would set out a programme only to be usurped by a man who knew nothing about sports science. The same was true of our chef, who at one point was told by the manager that he wasn't allowed to cook with salt any more. As they say, a little bit of knowledge can be a dangerous thing.

But then again, success and failure could well depend on which way a manager operates with this character trait. A friend who played for Chelsea under Mourinho told me that on a pre-season tour of America, the squad had been booked to do a photo shoot for their sponsor, Samsung. Upon hearing that Samsung hadn't provided any riders for the players, Mourinho promptly instructed his team to get back on the bus. After a lot of panicking, presumably by Samsung's PR department, it was agreed that a box packed full of electrical products would be waiting for each player upon their return to England. I have no idea whether that story is true but that's what this particular player told me and he has no reason to lie. I like to think that it is true because I quite like the cut of Mourniho's jib anyway, and if a manager did that for me, setting aside the freebies for a moment, I would instantly feel that we were all in it together and that he had my back. I would want to play for that man and do well for him.

That's not to say that players don't have responsibilities to their clubs. Companies such as Samsung pay a small fortune for the rights to exploit their sponsorship of Premier League football clubs and they have very tight contracts that make sure they get access to the players. Sometimes, however, it isn't always obvious – to the players at least – exactly what is going on around them.

I remember when I realised that a break we were enjoying somewhere near the equator was in fact nothing more than a massive networking exercise for our manager. The first clue that something peculiar was taking place came when we arrived at a brand new all-singing and all-dancing hotel slap bang on the sea front. We had our pictures taken with what felt like every one of the hotel's 1,500 staff before going for a swim in the sea to stave off the jet lag. That evening we were given dinner by some seriously wealthy hosts who, as it turned out, owned the restaurant we were in and had flown the whole squad out in business class.

These guys began to crop up again and again throughout our stay, and each time they did we were always in a restaurant, a shopping mall, a hotel or a nightclub that they owned, having our pictures taken under the place's signage. The patronage that our Premier League club afforded all of these companies must have been hugely valuable, so let me tell you what I think. I think that same manager goes back to that hotel every year for his holidays and will continue to do so until the day he dies. I am also willing to bet that he never pays for a single thing when he's out there. But I suppose that's business.

I have been dragged to just about every event you can imagine, having photographs taken in my club tracksuit and smiling like an idiot with no clue as to why I am there. On one occasion our squad spent the day walking around a manufacturing plant for home decor, signing autographs for all the workers. As far as I'm aware, none of the players received any home furnishings out of it – not that we needed any. Our manager probably didn't need any either at the time. But if he does in the future, I'm sure he'll be fine. This sort of thing probably happens at every level to varying degrees, but the difference between the squad turning a blind eye or coming to resent their manager could well lie in the success that the club enjoys on the pitch.

It's all about retaining the confidence of the players by treating them in a way that doesn't demean them. A friend of mine who used to play for Manchester United told me that even when he knew his time was up at Old Trafford, he was still treated with the same respect as anybody else in the squad. While that is not necessarily a rarity, it certainly isn't an approach adopted by every manager he and I have played under. The appreciation for what Sir Alex did for his career when it would have been far easier to do nothing at all is something that humbles my friend to this day. "I can still call him and I know he will spare me as much time as he can for a chat, and whether it's a week, a month or a year since we last talked, he remembers my kids' names and always asks after them."

For the record, another friend who currently plays for United always refuses to be drawn into conversation when I ask him about Ferguson, and is not backward in telling me that the reasons are fear, loyalty and respect, in any order you like.

Keeping the players on their toes is a high-wire act encompassing trust and respect and not, as one of my old managers thought, about organising as many nights out as possible, regardless of results, so that the players will like you more. A lot of players will abuse any sign of weakness in a manager and then find an excuse for their own failings when the team start to lose matches. I'm sure we can all think of a club that this applies to – they won the Champions League in 2012.

Managers are helped in their jobs by a few things that aren't for sale in any transfer window: resources, timing and luck, to name but three. Every manager leaves his mark, though, in one way or another. Years ago, one of my first managers took exception to a comment that was made by one of the players in the changing room after an away game. We had been hammered that day, not just in terms of the score but also in our general performance against a side that appeared to have signed a load of ringers.

After each match, the home team lays on tea and sandwiches for the away side, and these are generally waiting in the changing room when the final whistle goes. I think it's quite quaint that you can get almost the same tray of sandwiches at Old Trafford as those served up at the Colchester Community Stadium (for the record, Arsenal go above and beyond and provide chicken nuggets). Unfortunately for my team-mate, the sandwiches that day had been brought in on a metal platter that was within easy reach of our manager. Bending down, he picked it up with his left hand and Frisbeed it at a tremendous speed towards the head of the player who had dared to offer an explanation for our woeful performance. It missed him by a fraction of an inch and left a crater in the wall behind him, while covering him in plaster dust. I have to say that if that had been aimed at my head, that tray would have been returned with interest, but my friend just sat there, probably relieved, because God only knows what sort of damage would have been done to his face if he hadn't flinched.

The effects of such pressure can be seen in every changing room in the country on any given weekend. The tension is quite unbearable at times because, as we all know, football managers must be among the easiest people in the country to sack. Indeed, the former Leeds United manager Howard Wilkinson once said that there are only two types of manager: "those that have been sacked and those that will be sacked in the future".

When a manager really finds himself in the spotlight, it is amazing how much a good right-hand man can help. Decent coaches are worth their weight in gold but, in my view, are often not given the respect that they are entitled to. Too many coaches are successful at various clubs but then, for no obvious reason, fall out of the game because they can't get another job. Football is very incestuous in this respect, with managers tending to employ the same staff wherever they go. If a manager that I worked for as a coach suddenly fell out of the game, the chances are I would too. It's all very well the FA training more and more coaches to improve English football, but unless they know somebody in the game, it will be extremely difficult for them to break through at any level.

A good coach will have the respect of the players and be easy to approach about all manner of subjects. I have played under coaches who have every qualification under the sun but just can't get their message across. Sometimes they over-coach and the players (me especially) become bored and far less enthusiastic on the training pitch. Conversely, some coaches just click right away. I have played for some fantastic men whose approach transcends differences of age, background and attitude. You find yourself thinking, "This guy knows what he is doing", and the pace and standard of training pick up as the sessions are embraced.

I am often asked what I do in two hours of training and the honest answer is that it depends on the manager and the coach in charge at the time. After a 40-minute warm-up involving shuttle runs, running between poles, skipping over small hurdles and quick feet through rope ladders, all some coaches want to do is split the squad up and play keep-ball. After a while, this is simply mind-numbing. I had one coach who would play 11-a-side one touch on a full-size pitch and we'd walk off after an hour thinking, "What am I doing at this club?" That's why it can be exciting when a manager and his coaches are sacked. And when a manager is sacked, make sure you go into his office, thank him for his efforts and wish him luck because you never know when you might be working with him again.

Occasionally, however, a manager will not be helped by the actions of his players. A few years ago the team I was playing for were whisked away to a warmer climate for a mid-season break to recharge their batteries. Upon our arrival at the hotel at around 9pm, the manager spelled out the rules for the few days that we'd be staying there. "You can have one night out but not tonight – tonight everyone goes to bed. Training will start every morning at 9am sharp until 11am because after that it gets too hot. Now get to bed. Oh, and breakfast is compulsory." (They always say that.) Within 20 seconds of the hotel doors shutting, the group chat on my phone went into overdrive. "Where are we going, then?" "Everyone meet by the pool in 15 minutes and we'll find a way out." "Who's ordering the taxis?' "Does anyone have an iPhone charger – I've forgotten mine?" (That last one was me – I'm famous for that.)

We eventually convened in the hotel grounds by a hole in the hedge and when nobody was looking we scrambled through one at a time before hailing cabs with lots of arm waving and jumping around as frantically but as quietly as we could. Eventually we were all on our way into town, but after that... I really have no memory. I have been told, however, that at around 3am our coach located us in a karaoke bar and drove us all back to the hotel in the minivan that had been hired to take us to the training pitches the next day. He would have been well within his rights to tell the manager, and it probably would have been the largest collective fine in the history of football, or he could have sat us down and read us the riot act himself – but in the event he did nothing and because of that our respect for him went through the roof and training improved dramatically. Now I think about it, he could have been holding it over our heads for when he needed a favour but I prefer to think that he was just a decent guy; otherwise all us have been had.

It does pay to have everyone onside, but they don't all have to like each other. They just need to get on and work as hard as possible for one another on the pitch. And this is where a good captain really comes to the fore. Throughout my entire career, I have only disagreed with the appointment of one captain, and that was because he never stood up for us when we needed him to.

During the 20011-12 season, I read that the England armband was being passed around like a live grenade, but I have had the honour of a captaincy at club level and it's amazing how a little armband (infuriatingly put on upside down most of the time – how hard can it be?) can make you push your chest out with pride and feel a foot taller. As much as players pretend they don't care, secretly, deep down, almost everybody wants to be captain. So just how important is the captain? Well, if you're really lucky, he may just be the difference between success and failure.

A manager will select a captain who can act as a link between him and the dressing room. But where there are tensions between the squad and the club's hierarchy, the captain should always act in the interests of the players. From bonuses and player fines to club functions and time off, a good captain is the one player who concerns himself with the off-field politics of a football club.

When I am the captain I like to arrive early on a match day. Ten minutes before the teams take to the pitch to warm up (usually 2.20pm) the two captains are called to the referees' room for a chat not dissimilar to the one a boxing referee will have with two fighters. What started off as a way of handing in the team sheet (a heavy fine if it's even a minute late) has graduated to a talk from the ref about what he expects once the match is under way. After you shake hands with all the officials and then the other captain, the referee will say something like: "OK, lads. You're both old enough and ugly enough. Don't fuck me about: if you've got a problem just talk to me, yeah? If one of your players is behaving in an aggressive way to me, my colleagues or another player, then I expect you to sort it out before I have to, OK? Good luck." Followed by handshakes all round.

I played under one captain who had the armband by default after an injury to the manager's first choice. He accepted it in name only and set about commissioning the kit man to produce a personalised hybrid version. What he ended up with was a Tubigrip – the sort of thing you put around a sprained ankle – with a giant C handwritten in black marker pen. The new armband spanned the entire length of his upper arm. Some players are like that: they want everybody to know that they are captain while pretending it's no big deal. He lost a lot of respect after that stunt, mainly from me.

Strangely, the most successful side I played in had the most unappreciated captain. He was everything that players detest – selfish, and occasionally weak when we needed him most. On one occasion our club did not want to negotiate our bonuses. We had exhausted most of our bargaining power and on the day that we were due to sign (all bonuses have to be submitted to the league by a certain date) we only had one option left: boycott the team photo. This may sound like a hollow threat, but from a sponsorship and political point of view, it is a huge deal. On the morning of the photo shoot, we refused to change into the new kit. The chief executive pleaded with us, but we stood firm, all except one. Outside on the pitch, alone, stood our captain, in full kit and ready to go. At a time when we needed a leader he had sold us down the river. He was never forgiven, and from that moment he was shunned by the squad. Anything he tried to organise fell on deaf ears and any time he needed a favour he didn't get it.

The ideal captain can scream at his team-mates, disagree with the manager and still maintain a flawless relationship with each and every one, thanks to the respect in which he is held. My friend who played for United under Roy Keane once told me: "When I was a young pro, I was having a really tough time with my contract. I didn't have an agent and didn't know what to do. Keane went in to see Ferguson with me and sorted everything out for no other reason than he was the captain of the football club. The next day he was swearing at me for misplacing a pass out on the training pitch."

I'm proud to say that I have captained a professional team, but the politics of the role mean you can spend more time arranging things off the field than getting things right on it, and that's something I no longer have the hunger for. While, for me, there is no more important job on a football pitch, today there are definitely far more important things off it.

CHAPTER 3
FANS

The principle of "six degrees of separation" says that the world is a small place in which an individual can get to any other person in no more than six links. The Premier League, however, has always been a law unto itself and continues to prove that it is possible for tens of thousands of people to get to one player within 90 minutes.

An unremarkable match in the 2011-12 season at Craven Cottage will be remembered for the hand gesture that Liverpool's Luis Suárez appeared to offer to the home fans at the end of his side's 1-0 defeat by Fulham. What surprised me most was that Suárez's middle finger was raised in response to chants of "Cheat! Cheat!", giving the impression that the Uruguayan is a little sensitive around the edges, despite being more experienced than most when it comes to taking flak.

The crime itself is not particularly heinous but, by the same token, it doesn't exactly cover Suárez or football in glory. I gather there are people who are still offended by certain hand gestures, although I'd be surprised if many of them are to be found inside football stadiums.

The relationship between fans and players has undoubtedly suffered since the wages on the pitch spiralled out of proportion to the pay slips in the stands. Thankfully, serious flashpoints, such as Eric

Cantona's kung-fu kick at Selhurst Park or El-Hadji Diouf's deplorable spitting incidents, remain few and far between.

It is difficult to describe just how angry a player can become on the pitch. I have frightened myself by how worked up I've got because of silly things like derogatory singing and name-calling. Players are so well shielded away from the pitch that very often you can find yourself becoming a touch precious on it.

A good friend of mine who has since retired was forever holding forth on the hypocrisy of fans. His belief was that while supporters felt it was their right to chastise footballers, they had real problems when what they dished out got thrown back at them. The hole in the argument is that the fans are the ones paying, although a right back I played with would use that as a way of turning the tables. "Keep putting your money in my pocket, mate," was his stock response to abuse.

Much of what fans shout is lost on players but occasionally we hear things, although we like to pretend otherwise. In general play it is impossible to pick out anything because of the concentration required and the speed at which the match takes place, but players taking corners and throw-ins would be lying if they said they never hear the insults. Oddly enough, it's at some of the bigger stadiums such as Old Trafford and the Emirates, where the atmosphere can be subdued for long periods as fans wait to be entertained, that you can occasionally hear a personal taunt near the touchline. But this too is rare – especially at Manchester United, where it feels as if the front three rows are occupied by day trippers who might be just as happy somewhere else, rather than ardent football fans. All of which is great if you're part of the away team.

Much of what is shouted is in jest, and as soon as the fans see you look over at them and smile it breaks the ice and defuses the situation. That was what happened at a game I was playing in several years ago, when the crowd sang "Does your missus know you're here?" to a player who had just been photographed with a young lady who wasn't his wife. The player in question laughed along as soon as the chant started, and of course once he did that, the crowd stopped singing.

Sometimes, however, that response isn't enough. That's when the line becomes a little blurry.

I am often asked what's the worst thing I've ever heard shouted from the stands and, believe me, I've heard it all, from the hope that your kids will die of Aids to death threats and every conceivable insult about wives or girlfriends. I don't want to start bleating but what I do find odd is that it is now very easy to get sent off the pitch for foul and abusive language, yet much more difficult to get thrown out of a football stadium for the same thing. Clearly it is impossible to eject 30,000 fans for chanting something offensive in unison but we all see and hear outrageous remarks that go unpunished.

The other side of the coin is that football supporters can be wonderfully witty. It was impossible not to laugh when Chelsea supporters yelled "Shoot!" whenever Ashley Cole, who had been involved in an incident with an air-rifle at the training ground days earlier, picked up the ball.

The sort of stick that Suárez has received, not only at Fulham but elsewhere, owes much to his magnetic attraction to controversy. This was evident before he arrived in England and has since been reinforced, not least through the eight-match ban he received for racially abusing Patrice Evra at Anfield in October 2011. This is a player who took a bite out of an opponent while playing for Ajax and, on a much grander stage, proclaimed with warped glee that "the hand of God now belongs to me" after he denied Ghana a winning goal in the 2010 World Cup quarter-finals with a deliberate handball. The crime was not keeping the ball out, which every footballer I know would have done, but showing a complete lack of class in the aftermath.

What is clear to me is that when a player reacts to abuse from the stands, it sends a message to fans up and down the country that he, and the rest of us, can be easily provoked.

As much as supporters are the lifeblood of a club and can even be a factor when players are deciding which club to sign for, if you can find a footballer who is willing to talk frankly, the chances are that it will not be long before he says: "Fans are clueless." While I don't entirely agree with that sentiment, I do understand where players are coming from. Unless you have played football full-time, then some things, no matter how well a player tries to explain them, will always remain the province of the professional.

One thing that frustrates players where fans are concerned is their attitude to keeping the ball. Sometimes when I'm injured or suspended, I'll sit in the stands to watch the game and it never ceases to amaze me what some fans shout during the match. Nothing annoys players more than the calls to "just get it up there". It seems that some people still don't appreciate the value of keeping the ball for what looks like no reason – and, worryingly, this is not confined to supporters.

Let's take England's passing statistics for Euro 2012. England's top passer, with 45 in one game, was Joe Hart against Italy. In that same match Andrea Pirlo completed 117 passes. What was equally depressing was Roy Hodgson's analysis of the match. "I don't regard possession statistics as particularly important," the England coach said.

So let me offer a few thoughts of my own. Ball retention at any level is important for four reasons. Firstly, when a team has the ball, the opposition can't score. Secondly, their opponents run themselves into the ground trying to get the ball back, and when they do gain possession they're too tired to do anything meaningful with it. Thirdly, the team controlling the ball is able to probe for an opening, often after dragging a player out of position by moving the ball quickly. Finally, keeping hold of the ball is the best way to recover. As a case in point, take a look at the state of the England players towards the end of normal time against Italy.

Thankfully, the message seems to be getting through to our next generation of players. Stand on the side of almost any academy match these days and the chances are you will hear a coach shout to his players just after they've won the ball back: "Rest in possession!" Not so long ago, Charles Hughes, a former schoolteacher who was charged with reinventing the English game, put forward the theory of Pomo – positions of maximum opportunity – which basically entailed bypassing the midfield and getting the ball to the front man as quickly as possible.

In many ways we are all being re-educated. I have always thought that a good example of our respective expectations can be glimpsed each time a player balloons a shot over the crossbar. In Italy and Spain there are whistles and jeers to make it clear that the standard on show isn't good enough. In this country when the same thing happens there is an "Ooooh", as if it was something to be admired. It also staggers me that people applaud two of the easiest passes to execute in football – the header to the goalkeeper from a defender who is under absolutely no pressure and the 20-yard sideways pass from the centre of midfield to the wide man.

The other side of the coin is that fans can panic players into making poor decisions. The more unsettled a crowd gets, the worse the football on show will become – I've seen it a million times. Certain grounds have a reputation. Whenever I've played at Wolverhampton Wanderers or West Ham United, every manager has said: "Keep this lot quiet for 20 minutes, and their fans will start getting on their back." By the same token, when your fans are right behind you, there is nothing better. It's that point when you've had a sustained period of pressure, maybe three or four corners in quick succession, and the noise levels are cranked up – you can see the opposition becoming nervous and your own team appears to grow. You find an extra yard of pace and seem to be first to every ball.

Fans can also be intimidating for very different reasons. Not so long ago I was playing in a match where I knew a lot of the opposition players. During a break in play for an injury, I began to chat with one of the players that I knew. Suddenly he hit the deck. I had looked away at the moment he'd crumpled to the ground and, fearing the worst, I bent down to help him, only to see a 50 pence piece by his side. It had come out of the crowd and caught him plum on the forehead – a tremendous shot and something a sniper would have been proud of. I saw the player afterwards and he had a pretty mean cut that will probably remind him of something he'd rather forget every time he goes to the mirror.

I thought it spoke volumes that he didn't complain. He didn't say anything to the stewards or the police who line the tunnel after each game. Either he didn't want to kick up a fuss or, more likely, he knew nothing would be done about it and he'd risk becoming a target at away games for being a crybaby.

Years earlier I had been lucky enough to play at the Den, home of Millwall. Believe me, that is a hostile crowd. After the match, three of us made our way to the coach, which for some reason was parked on the other side of the car park. As we walked, a group of four or five heavily set men came the other way. One had his son with him, who couldn't have been more than seven years old. He was jogging every so often so as to keep up with the adults. It reminded me of myself with my dad and that habit he had of walking twice as fast outside football stadiums, as the adrenaline took over. As we got closer I was able to make out the tattoos that littered each man's arms. Fearing the worst, I continued shuffling and fixed my focus firmly on the ground. As we got closer, I could feel that all of them were looking at us and I waited for the abuse to start. Just when I thought we were in the clear the little boy looked up at us and said to the player on my right: "Nigger!" I remember being absolutely horrified. The player in question let out a laugh somewhere between disbelief and shock. Nobody said anything and everybody carried on walking. I don't know which was worse – hearing this from a child or that his father didn't bat an eyelid.

The point, though this is an extreme case, is that much of what a child learns comes directly from his or her parents. They are the closest influence and a guide to acceptable behaviour. This is why I struggle to accept the idea of footballers as role models. While I'm not condoning some of the things that players do, if your son or daughter is copying them, ask yourself why they're taking more notice of a Premier League footballer than they are of you, or why you expose them to some of the most disgusting abuse they could ever hear.

It doesn't get any more disgusting than racism, which during the 2011-12 season reared its ugly head on the pitch and at the highest level. As much as we like to think that we've come a long way in this country since the days of banana-throwing and monkey chants, the truth is that racism is still a problem. This may alarm some people, but at every club I've been at there has been a black player and a white player who have their own unique relationship, which at times leads to them making racist remarks to each other that nobody else in the changing room could get away with. Yes, the players involved are laughing with each other, but for me that doesn't make it right.

Of course, it was a very different set of circumstances at Anfield with Evra and Suárez. The punishment that Suárez received sent out a strong message and, although I've made it clear where I stand on the idea that footballers carry more influence than parents, I'd be the first to admit that we have a responsibility to ourselves, our fellow professionals, our clubs and the wider public when it comes to setting the bar for what is and is not acceptable. And when it comes to racism, there is no other way than zero tolerance.

While plenty of effort has been made to tackle racism, we simply haven't had much opportunity to deal with homophobia, another of football's taboo subjects. When it is mentioned, it usually triggers a spate of absurd media debates in an all-too-predictable attempt to uncover why the newspapers, TV, radio and websites have no gay footballer to chew up and spit out. Just look at the question put to Antonio Cassano during Euro 2012, when the Italy striker was asked about media reports that there were two "metrosexual" players and two homosexual players in the Italy squad. While Cassano's answer – "Queers in the national team? That's their business. But I hope not" – was deplorable, what business is it of anyone else what someone's sexuality is?

By the law of averages, it is highly likely that there are more gay players in professional football than Anton Hysén, the Swede who came out in 2011. That said (and with apologies for the appalling stereotyping here), anyone watching players arriving at a match for the first time could be forgiven for thinking the game was played exclusively by homosexual men, such is the attention paid to hair placement, general attire and luxury washbags. Don't get me started on some of the things I have seen produced from the latter.

I don't "officially" know any gay footballers, although I suspect I have been only a Jägerbomb or two away from a team-mate confiding in me. What we are all agreed on, however, is that there is one very good reason that gay players would keep their sexual allegiance firmly in the locker: the fans. Most football supporters limit themselves to relatively harmless banter. But increasingly, it seems, an element are being allowed to cross the line. From abusing players for their skin tone to their nationality, certain fans will grab hold of anything if they can get a cheap laugh and be able to tell their mates down the pub what they shouted out during the game.

It takes an awful lot to sicken me on a football pitch, probably because I have heard it all before. There is one man at a London club who shouts the same thing at me from the same seat every season I play there. Now I just smile and he laughs, happy that I have heard him, but it certainly didn't start out that way. After the first few times I got so fed up that as the ball was bouncing away towards the touchline I took aim with a lethal left-footed volley (he sits near to the front), missing him by inches. You can imagine the abuse he gave me for missing him after that.

Unfortunately, while I am now hardened, others are still forming their protective shell. A few years ago I saw a talented young kid reduced to tears in the changing room because of the abuse he took from a couple of buffoons. He never told anyone what was said and nobody ever asked him – but, thinking back, I can guess.

So would you come out and then travel around the country playing football in front of tens of thousands of people who hate you? I wouldn't. I would be in the dressing room feeling hugely depressed that certain components of our great game make it all but impossible for me to do anything other than keep quiet. I would also have in mind the gay footballer Justin Fashanu, who tragically took his own life in 1998.

Football has moved on since then... or has it? Rewind to Fratton Park, September 2008, when Sol Campbell was subjected to homophobic abuse and a section of Spurs supporters were caught on film singing: "Sol, Sol, wherever you may be, Not long now until lunacy, We won't give a fuck if you are hanging from a tree, You are a Judas cunt with HIV." Apologies if you didn't like reading those words. But spare a thought for how Campbell felt when he was listening to them.

Sadly, I'd say the general abuse players receive hasn't got much better. Very rarely is there any appreciation of the opposition's great play: a stunning goal is normally met with a thousand hand gestures from the stands, and our best talent is routinely booed with a vigour and hatred that, I feel, offers us a precious insight into society as a whole.

Having said all of that, I'm pretty sure a gay player would have few problems coming out to his team-mates if he were offered a magic "Nobody outside the team will ever find out" guarantee. It isn't because we're a superior breed – even I wouldn't take on that argument with half the England team conspiring against me. It is because we're all about looking after ourselves and, consequently, we try not to get too involved with other players' trials and tribulations. That said, there is a tremendous sense of camaraderie each time a player is targeted by the media, the fans or another team. In some cases that loyalty is probably abused, which is what we saw in the wake of the Suárez-Evra incident, when the Liverpool players wore T-shirts in support of a team-mate who had been found guilty of racially abusing another professional.

The changing room is a harsh place to survive – say what you like about footballers' lack of intelligence (and people often do), the banter is razor-sharp and anything out of the ordinary is seized upon in a flash. But this is precisely why a gay player would feel comfortable coming out here. A footballer is a footballer: it doesn't matter if you are black, white, straight or gay. Players are at ease in this environment, where they are used to piss-taking.

But the terraces are a different ball game. We are very much on our guard around fans.

Footballers have learned to cope with a huge amount of stick from the terraces, and mostly this is because we know there is little chance of anyone hurdling the barrier to make their point in a more physical manner. The field is treated as a kind of protective force field in that respect. Except, perhaps, on derby day.

Rivalry in football is nothing new but it could be argued that the animosity has grown as the stakes have become higher. In the run-up to a grudge match or derby game, the sense of anticipation around town is inescapable. During the build-up to one of these fixtures, I can recall almost every person I met greeting me with the words: "Make sure you win on Sunday." People say this to me anyway, but ahead of this particular game it felt like more of a threat, such was the bad blood between the fans.

As a rule, such games are not particularly enjoyable for the players. The hatred I sometimes saw can perhaps best be summed up by the last five minutes of one game against our fiercest rivals. Losing and desperate for a goal, we began to take chances by committing as many men forward as possible. Eventually we mustered a shot that ended up in the stand, among our own supporters, for a goal kick. The ball, however, did not come back. More than anything else that went on in that derby, the fact that not one of our fans could bring themselves to throw the ball back to the rival goalkeeper, even though we were losing and running out of time, says a lot about the hatred that they had for a team that they were desperate to beat.

Off the pitch, my relationship with the fans has been up and down. I've found that people are a lot braver when they are in a group than on their own; for that reason I try to leave the match with someone who happens to be playing well at the time. But there have been times when I have had to put up a physical defence of my good name in the face of a backlash from supporters. I remember being cornered in a nightclub by four inebriated meatheads and having to blindly punch my way to the door where I knew the bouncers would be waiting. And it is these nights out that are the real danger for both fans and players.

The simple truth is that I expect there to be trouble on a night out, because people tend to have a fair amount to drink and, as a result, suddenly become very brave or very stupid. For a professional footballer, it is easy to divide the opinion of a roomful of people without speaking to any of them. Personally, I try to avoid nights out with big groups of lads. For years I even managed to skip the Christmas party until the announcement that we would be fined if we didn't attend.

In five years at one of my clubs, my girlfriend and I had no more than a dozen nights out – and they were always for something to eat, and usually for someone's birthday. Leaving aside the possibility of violence, I don't like getting into conversations because I am hugely paranoid that I am being recorded. The technology on mobile phones means that everyone is a journalist now.

When I started out in football, I had no idea of the lengths people would go to to talk to me, argue with me, or try to engage me in a fight. After a while it simply became too much aggravation to step out of the front door. It isn't the nights out that are the problem for me because, on the whole, they are easily sidestepped. It is the day-to-day things that fill me with dread. At one point, shopping for groceries became a bizarre experience as people followed me around looking at what I put in my basket. I even saw someone copying me, which makes me think I'm responsible for a mini-boom in the sales of Frosted Shred-dies (other breakfast cereals are available).

Much of what I encounter is harmless, but I'm always on my toes these days because I've learned people will ask for anything and every-thing. The first time it happened, I thought the guy concerned was taking the piss when he asked if I could get him a trial at my club. He looked like he was closing in on 40 and something told me (the size of his waist was a clue) that there was a reason he had slipped through the net.

But before I knew it, I was in possession of his mobile phone number, his home address and his place of work. In other words, he was deadly serious. I remember talking to the older profession-als about it when I went into training and they laughed at me. The captain said: "You need to develop your stock answers, lad." I had no idea what he was on about but today my responses are honed. The trick is to reply instantly and never waver. "Write to the club – they'll tell you everything you need to know," in response to a dad asking if I can recommend his kid for a trial. "I'm sorry – it says in our contract that we can't do that," in reply to a group of lads asking if I can play in their five-a-side team or turn out for a game on Sunday morning for the Dog and Duck.

During the nights out that I can't wriggle out of, the worst I usually have to deal with is earache from lads who make me feel too old to be there in the first place. I always try to leave before the fighting starts. But almost every time I go out, I can guarantee that a young bloke will, at some point, shout something along the lines of "This geezer is going to be the next Wayne Rooney. Crewe have just offered him an apprenticeship" in my ear. This comes from the boy wonder's best mate, while Crewe's latest academy recruit stands next to him with a bottle of Corona in each hand, dressed as an extra from Footballers' Wives and pretending he doesn't know who I am or what his friend is talking about.

You never know when these people will strike, so it pays to have a solid, inoffensive stock answer to fall back on, in part so you don't find yourself tripping over your words and agreeing to something you can't get out of. I am always firm but I make sure that I'm never rude. "Good luck at Crewe – it's a great club. Go easy on the beers." And then, for reasons I don't understand, I'll buy them each a drink.

As my career has progressed, I have adopted a pretty severe solution to avoiding the people who want my time. I have stopped going out. I can't even do big crowds at shopping centres because they make me feel anxious (pretty embarrassing, really, although I get enough shit on a Saturday, so the idea of being abused outside Starbucks isn't particularly appealing). And I don't like going anywhere where I think I may end up fending off questions like: "Is so-and-so a prick? How much money is he on? And can you get me two tickets?"

What I will say, though, is that there is no feeling like having tens of thousands of fans singing your name, especially when you have just scored a goal. It feels as if you are floating for a couple of seconds. You don't hear anything that the players are shouting in your ear as they try to celebrate with you. Do you remember the moment in Saving Private Ryan where a bomb goes off near Tom Hanks and he is momentarily dazed and deaf? It is similar to that. It is just a wall of colour for a few seconds as your brain attempts to find a pattern that it understands. When the whistle goes to get the game under way again, it feels as if you can do anything for about a minute afterwards. When I finish playing, that might just turn out to be the one thing that I can't replace.

CHAPTER 4
THE MEDIA

I have had some disastrous experiences with tabloid journalists. Something appears to go terribly wrong between the last question being asked and the copy appearing in the newspaper the following day, so that what feels like a friendly and innocuous interview is twisted into something totally different.

In fairness, they are not all like this. Most interviews that fall outside of press conferences are conducted with a club official in the room, who vets the questions and strikes any answers from the record that may be detrimental to the club or the player. But if you are collared by a journalist outside the training ground, then you take your reputation into your own hands – especially if the journalist is freelance and selling stories with controversy as the main hook. I'm also uncomfortable when journalists rely on shorthand rather than dictaphones, because it ends up becoming your word against theirs when a questionable story appears.

During my career, I have been stitched up for many things. Far and away the most bizarre was to do with my supposed addiction to methadone, which, as all you budding doctors reading this will know, is a replacement drug usually given to heroin addicts in an attempt to wean them off the junk. I first found out that this story was building when a friend who lives in America called to say that "a British guy from one of the red-tops" wanted to ask her what she knew about my dependency on the drug. The background to all this was that I'd had an operation a few weeks before and, as a result, was taking some pretty heavy-duty prescription pain relief. I mentioned to a journalist at the local rag that the pills had become life savers because of the amount of pain I was in. From there, the Chinese whispers began. My friend didn't say anything to the guy on the other end of the phone but that didn't stop his newspaper from trying to run a story the very next day suggesting I had overdosed on painkillers.

I'd like to say this was a one-off but it wasn't. Stories like this would just appear as if by magic, with very tenuous connections to the truth. On another occasion, I had a legitimate phone call from a manager who asked me if I would consider playing for his team. I politely declined as I was very happy where I was. The next day he tried again: "If we could get to about £35k a week would you sign?" So, naturally, I said that at that figure there would certainly be a conversation to be had. I thanked him for his call and hung up. The next day, a national paper ran a piece that held me up as its poster boy for "the kind of mercenaries that are ruining the game in this country". Clearly the second phone call had come from a journalist masquerading as the manager. To put it bluntly, I went fucking ape-shit and threatened so much legal action against that newspaper that we'd probably still be going through the courts today had we not agreed to settle. I still didn't get an apology.

But we are not always the victims. Footballers are fantastic fodder for the papers. We are their favourite kind of celebrity: young, wealthy and often full of attitude. It's not entirely surprising that we have migrated from their back pages to the front.

If the theory of evolution tells us anything, it is that all males have an almost uncontrollable instinct to procreate. This particular force of nature appears to be so strong that it can deliver the most successful of men in our line of work into the arms of celebrity-obsessed young women. If evolution hinges on the previous generation improving on the last, then I suppose even nature is occasionally flawed.

I haven't worked for a club that hasn't had a player caught out by his girlfriend or wife. But, on the other hand, there are plenty of footballers' partners who turn a blind eye to indiscretions because they know that the life they enjoy would disappear if they walked out. I know wives who have walked in on their other half when he's in full swing, gone shopping, come home and had his dinner on the table as if nothing had happened. They simply cannot do without a designer wardrobe, two weeks in Dubai and half of Tiffany's every Christmas and birthday, and so look the other way.

This amicable agreement that dare not speak its name only becomes a problem when the media get hold of it. Even then, the general rule is that things are brushed under the carpet as quickly as possible. The exception is when a wife no longer needs the player.

Please don't think I've got a downer on all women. I know there are lots of honest, decent ones who aren't driven by a love of luxury or prestige – I'm lucky enough to have married one – but many of those who gravitate towards professional footballers are less admirable.

Affairs have been going on since life on earth began, but they really became something for footballers to worry about when the media began to pay out five- and six-figure sums for stories. It always amazed me on nights out how many players would end up sleeping with a girl they'd known for just five minutes, when they could be setting themselves up for tomorrow's headline.

It's no secret why footballers are so sought-after for a quick one between the sheets. They are seen as trophies among certain girls, not least the groupies who I see hanging around outside the training ground and try to avoid as if they have the plague. When you factor in the chance that they will sell their story or are under the delusion that the two of you will live together happily ever after, you're best off without them. Unless you are single, in which case you take your pick. I've met some prolific shaggers who will go to extraordinary lengths to get their end away. Some "urgent medical appointments" take place in bizarre locations at very strange times of the day.

The real question is: what's in it for the player? After all, the risk and reward are completely out of sync. A married player has so much to lose for the sake of five minutes of lust. But it's more than that. There is the bravado. I can sit down with a stunning woman and she'll hang on my every word; I can make the worst jokes and she'll laugh like I'm a stand-up; I can buy her bottles of champagne and she'll be impressed. In short, a player can have his ego stroked relentlessly, sleep with a beautiful woman at the end of it and, nine times out of 10, he'll get away with it. If, indeed, his wife or regular girlfriend even cares.

There is another reason for some of what goes on. Many players have childhood sweethearts who they end up marrying, and many of them will have kids at a young age before they have had the chance to "sow their oats", as some might say. When a player begins to earn the big bucks, that's when the temptations really start: they coincide with the arrival of the Louis Vuitton handbags and the first-class flights to Barbados. I see this situation occasionally as new players and their girlfriends join the club, barely able to hold a conversation at first. Two years in, the kids are with a nanny, the wife is on the phone to Cartier and the player is in a hotel room licking Cristal off a.... well, you get the idea.

The rise of the Wag has not helped the situation. Some of these creatures (which doesn't sound particularly flattering but is how they have come to be known in the trade) are obsessed by fame. At one club I used to play for they had a column in the programme called something like "Meet the Wags". To the question "Who do you look up to?", all of them replied either Victoria Beckham or Katie Price. Now, there isn't anything wrong with that per se, because both of those women are very successful in business; but I am convinced that this was not the reason for the answers. It is because they live a lifestyle that the Wags are, generally, desperate to emulate. They design handbags, wear top labels and have celebrity husbands, fast cars and houses all over the planet.

It is no different from the youth team players of today living well beyond their means and buying the most expensive watch, car and so on that they can afford. They are emulating what they see in the newspapers, and not what they see on the pitch. Frank Lampard had a strong take on this a few years ago: "The lads are forgetting the hard work that needs to be done to earn this sort of lifestyle. Not enough of them have the same dedication, and it's something I feel very strongly about. They think they have made it already." Don't get me wrong:

cleaning boots is no substitute for talent, but it certainly helps to keep you grounded and, arguably, appreciate the trappings that hard work and dedication can bring.

The combination of all these factors is manna from heaven for the newspapers. The Wags are desperate to be in the papers, and so are the young professionals. The difference between today and how it was when I was coming up is that the youth team players want to be on the front page, not the back.

A friend who used to play football with me years ago and has since retired told me a great story from when he was in Dubai at the One and Only resort. He and his wife had checked in at the same time as another player, who is now an international, and *his* wife. You all know him, though his wife is probably more famous than him in certain circles. My friend, who, it has to be said, is a handsome bastard (which would make him very dislikable if he wasn't such a nice bloke), was sunning himself at one end of the swimming pool. The One and Only's main pool is surrounded on all sides by hundreds of sun loungers full of people who my wife refers to as "frightful shits" – it is extremely busy.

While my friend was working up a tan, he noticed the wife of the other player slip into the water at the far end of the pool. It wasn't long before she began to do a few strokes – and not the ones that go from one end of the pool to the other. My friend said that after he had caught her eye a couple of times she made a beeline for him. When she was close enough, she wrapped her legs around him and reached down to... well, as I say, perform a few strokes. Her husband was asleep on a sun lounger under a shady tree.

When I put it to him that what he was telling me was in fact nothing more than complete bullshit, he looked offended before bringing out his mobile phone to show me a few of the picture messages that she'd sent him after their return. And very well manicured she was too, may I say. The following week some pictures of the couple appeared in one of the glossy magazines but this time she had her clothes on.

Anyone who had taken a picture of the action in the pool would have made a fortune and at the same time made four lives unbearable for a time. In fairness that fact was not lost on my friend, but he still had a rather pragmatic take on the situation when I suggested he was an idiot. "I know it's stupid," he told me. "Everyone knew who she was and they were all looking –but it's *her*, isn't it?"

I once witnessed a fellow player spill out of a hotel lobby in Newcastle with a beautiful woman on his arm. Nothing too exciting there, until I realised that this was the same women who the previous night had droned on and on to anyone who would listen about her three kids, her husband and how she loved teaching at the local primary school. I thought my friend was banging his head against a brick wall and I told him so. I actually wanted him to leave her alone because I've seen, too many times, how these innocent chats are anything but. But he saw her as a challenge. A few Jägerbombs later and her kids couldn't have been further from her mind. With all the single women out there, this "I will because I can" attitude from the footballer in question doesn't sit right with me. And if a player is caught out in these circumstances, then as far as I'm concerned it's a fair cop.

No footballer who preaches ethics where the media are concerned, especially those who ply their trade in the Premier League, would be foolish enough to completely regret the influence they have in this country. After all, Sky TV has pumped billions of pounds into football, which in turn has filtered down into our pockets. Personally, I don't have a huge issue with Sky. I don't entirely subscribe to the theory that money has ruined football, even if it has probably contributed to England's repeated failures in major tournaments. What I have always had a problem with, though, is the tabloid press in this country.

As a schoolkid, I did my work experience at our local newspaper. I was seduced by the idea of raincoat-clad hacks stumbling from the Cheshire Cheese yelling "Hold the front page!" as an inebriated source let his guard down over an MP and his mistress. The reality, I'm afraid to say, was hour after hour of sheer boredom, the occasional tea run and long bus journeys to meet elderly widows who had won £1,000 on the pools. I could be wrong, but I think the shattering of that illusion fed my distrust of tabloid reporters. (Not that I think the broadsheets are any better; it is simply that we don't have as much interaction with them in our world, save the occasional "feature" piece.)

When I first came into professional football, all the senior players, to a man, warned me off the media. "Don't talk to them if you can avoid it. And if you do speak to them, never tell them anything more than you absolutely have to," my captain said at the time. I had always seen the media as a chance to put myself in the shop window. The more I was in the papers and on television, I reasoned, the more my name would stick with those within the game. I have since seen some average players get big moves, apparently on this basis. I include myself there. The theory was sound enough, but the continuing execution has been patchy at best.

My initial exposure to the media was on a local level. At my first club, the local paper had a hack whom I shall call Bernie. Bernie carried himself in a manner that suggested he was the best friend you never had and that you could confide anything that might be on your mind. I have to say that the dark art of soliciting information that some journalists practise can be quite impressive when you're not on the end of it. Bernie had been told that "this kid" – I – had a real chance in the game and would one day be worth a lot of money to the club by way of a transfer fee. Because of this I was off limits unless there was a representative of the club sitting in on the interview (something that is the norm at most clubs these days).

Two weeks in, Bernie made his move.

"How does it feel to know that the manager holds you in such high regard?" he asked.

"It's flattering. I have lots to learn. I'm honoured to be at the club..." I replied.

"How do you feel about the manager predicting you'll have a big future in the game?"

"It's flattering. Let's hope he's right."

"What club did you support as a boy?"

"Liverpool."

Monday's headline: "[The Secret Footballer] can't wait to hit the big time." The story continued: "[Club X] are weighing up a £1m move for [the Secret Footballer] but will need to beat off strong competition for his signing from the player's preferred destination... Liverpool.'

I'd like to say that I learned quickly, but that would be bullshit. As the seasons have slipped by I have been caught out by every conceivable hack trick in the book, probably because I am pretty decent value in an interview. I don't insist on having an official from the club sitting on my shoulder – something that irritates journalists. (To be fair, this doesn't always turn out badly. I have a good friend at one paper who, after I'd given him a very frank interview, didn't stitch me up. I still have the piece he did because of that.)

The longer you play, the more contacts you'll make. It is a naive player who does not keep tabs on who's who in the world of newspaper journalism. You never know when you will need to call on somebody for a favour. And very often, your favour will be their front page. Even if you do fuck up, the report will be less damning if you have previously befriended the journalist.

An example of this came a few years ago when I was suffering from a couple of spectacular fall-outs with my manager. We hadn't seen eye to eye on a few things during my stay with the club and this came to a head after a high-profile match. We exchanged views during the game, because I felt I was being made the scapegoat for our bad performance. What also grated with me was that a couple of months earlier, "Paolo", our maverick foreign striker, had stepped out of line for the umpteenth time and got away with it yet again.

The day after the game, the manager called the whole squad in and told us that, from now on, anyone who showed him up in public would be fined two weeks' wages. And then, turning to me, he said: "You got that? You have a fucking problem, then you come and see me. My door is always open." To which I replied, "Gaffer, I assure you, should I ever want to speak to you, then you will be the first to know." And that about summed up our relationship at that point.

The vibration of my phone on the bedside cabinet woke me the following morning. I was inundated with messages asking me whether I had seen one of the tabloid newspapers that day. I don't buy tabloids and so I took my usual slowish journey to the training ground with that feeling of impending doom tightening around my chest with every mile covered, knowing that there would be a few half-read copies of the paper in question waiting for me in the canteen. As I pulled up and stepped out of the car I was met by the shouts of a dozen players who had lined up outside the changing rooms to await my arrival. "Here he is!" "Bad boy!" "Quick, hide!" (I still don't understand that last one.) They couldn't wait to stick a copy of the paper in my hands.

Inside the back cover was a double-page spread that was probably close to what my manager would have commissioned if, for some reason, he'd been given the editor's job for the day. There were quotes aplenty, all of which pretty much denounced what I stood for, what I'd achieved in the game, and my motivation for playing football. It was hard reading, but only because it was complete and utter bullshit. I'm not a particularly violent man but if my manager had been close by, it's fair to say things would have become physical.

My main reason for keeping in contact with journalists who have interviewed me during my career (and not stitched me up) is obvious: should I ever need to bite someone, really hard and where it hurts, then it is only ever a phone call away. A very well-known friend of mine who writes for a respected newspaper was only too happy to deliver my riposte. Within two days the world knew the truth about this manager and why what he had said about me was a lie. The piece was so good that I keep it safely in my office. For a long time I used it as a guide and the benchmark when structuring my Secret Footballer columns for the Guardian. I have never got anywhere near the standard that the journalist set but it has certainly helped.

Where using the media to my advantage is concerned, that episode remains my crowning glory and although my time at the club thereafter was extremely awkward, I didn't care. It was worth it. I had shown that I was not a yes man and, more importantly, both of us now knew that if ever he tried anything like that again, I had just as many friends in the media as he did. And that alone can be a valuable commodity in this game. You only have to look at the way the media reacted to the news that Roy Hodgson had been appointed to the England job ahead of Harry Redknapp, the newspapers' favourite manager.

So far as I know, Bernie is still at the local paper, still writing about the same club. I don't think it was his intention to stitch anyone up, not properly anyway. I think he simply loved the hustle and bustle of the whole industry. For him, it was about getting the story into print as quickly as possible before he moved on to the next one, ducking and diving to get the scoop with little thought for the consequences. Actually, I think he really missed the frantic pace of working for a big city newspaper. I guess it's a bit like playing football: once you've been to the top, anything else is a poor second. Looking back, it's obvious why I liked Bernie despite his attempts to flog me and every other player at the club. In his own way he was very similar to me. I will stop at nothing to cut someone down to size and Bernie had a similar determination to get his story out before anybody else, no matter who he upset along the way,

As my career took off I left Bernie behind but, as with almost every person that I have met in football, he taught me a lesson. It may sound obvious but if you slip up in football the newspapers will publish it. You can't have friends where some journalists are concerned – only acquaintances.

At my next club, I met a journalist who certainly sharpened my wits. When I signed, even the chairman warned me not to talk to him (presumably he'd been stitched up at some point). A few of the older players told me that a group of fans had set upon him outside some shops in a rougher part of town and given him a severe beating. I never did find out what that was about but if the fans were turning on him, then you knew he couldn't be trusted.

This was a big club and the journalist in question was feeding stories into the national press in return for a fee. This is very normal but it seemed that every little thing that went on at our club found its way into the national press. While I was there, several stories involving death threats, drink driving, overdoses and assault went nationwide. To anyone on the outside looking in, we must have seemed like the ultimate problem club. Nothing could have been further from the truth. Whenever I go back to that club I refuse all interviews, just to spite that idiot.

But that isn't to say that he wasn't deliberately fed with some spectacular tabloid fodder. As our club hit a boom, things began to change out of all recognition. The previously under-the-radar wives and girlfriends became Wags almost overnight and would start to drop their men at the training ground in brand-new Range Rovers, on the offchance that a photographer would be there to snap them.

One of these "creatures" actually had the nerve to ask my better half to call her Queen Wag (yes, seriously). I saw her at the Cheltenham Festival recently and although she saw me, she didn't smile, wave or say anything. Just as well, because I've forgotten her real name.

We felt the impact of success almost immediately. There were police cars waiting for us as we left the training ground, and I think every player was pulled over at least once for misdemeanours ranging from a faulty brake light to using a mobile while driving. I was followed home regularly, presumably to see if I'd commit a traffic violation. It was a crazy time and of course all of this turned up in the press.

Playing Premier League football is a dream come true, but away from the pitch I would happily swap almost everything. The aggravation from all sides is too much to deal with at times, and the frustration at not being able to say how you feel for fear of being stitched up and having your quotes "twirled", as they say in the trade, is something that I struggled with. Because of that, I tend to bottle everything up before giving one big interview where I'll let everything out, then retreat and wait for the fallout.

But you can't have one without the other. During the transfer windows the media can be vital. Agents use them to tease an offer out of a preferred club by making out there is interest from another team. You know all those rumours that you read in the back of the paper? That's all the majority of them are – agent talk. The player involved in them might be on the move but the team that the paper is quoting is, more often than not, a red herring. It's the oldest trick in the agent's Filofax and amazingly it still works from time to time. In the early days of the Sky News 24-hour sports channel it was notoriously easy to get stories on to the tracker bar at the bottom; a few of us used to do it while sitting in our digs. The players would dare each other to ring in with a fabricated story while passing on the number of an "agent", who was actually another player. Somebody from Sky would phone to check the story and before you could say, "Wayne Rooney to Grimsby on a three-year deal" it was scrolling along the breaking news bar at the bottom. These days it would be impossible to pull the same stunt.

On the back of the money that Sky has invested in Premier League football, there are opportunities for players to continue to play a role in the game, albeit as commentators and pundits. Indeed, the £40,000 a show that Match of the Day pundit Alan Hansen is reputed to earn makes punditry about as sought-after as a first-team position for a top-flight club. Whenever I have an injury I am often asked to "do the matchday media". This involves either co-commentary or interviews with local papers (nationals tend to want somebody who was playing, while locals are just happy to get anyone to talk about their own situation, simply because they need to fill their newspaper for the whole week).

Punditry is something that I have thought very hard about. I have gone on record as saying that I wouldn't be interested until a new avenue opens up that I think I'd be more suited to. For example, years ago nobody would have dreamed that a media outlet would have an army of ex-players traipsing up and down the country reporting on the weekend's matches, on television but with no footage of the action. But that's exactly what happens today. Furthermore, Gary Lineker has shown that an ex-player can be comfortable broadcasting across multiple genres, while Gary Neville has added a wealth of knowledge to Sky after he replaced the tired and out-of-touch Andy Gray. On the other hand, Robbie Savage has proven to all that it is just as easy to make a fool of yourself on the football pitch, on the dance floor and as a pundit. And still get paid for it.

I have said before that it is a waste of knowledge simply to retire from football and live a different dream. While that was in reference to coaching (far too much knowledge is wasted when top players retire), I am less certain about where to impart the knowledge that I have learned. On the one hand I have always wanted to coach academy kids, but there is next to no money in it unless you can tie up with an agency that represents the kids. Personally, I feel that is a conflict of interests, but that's not to say that it doesn't happen a lot. On the other hand, punditry, which is my second choice, pays pretty well. When broadcasters started to ask me to appear on a regular basis, I would turn them down on the grounds that too much airtime would lead to people asking why I wasn't playing. In my view, it is best to keep out of the limelight if you are not in the team. The catch, however, is that if an injury has put paid to playing, a reduction in bonuses is certain to follow. There are no appearance fees or win bonuses and, depending on what type of contract a player has, that will be reflected in his pay packet.

Eventually the BBC offered me its standard £400 fee for services rendered (co-commentary), which I gratefully accepted. I enjoyed the experience and would happily do it again, even though I have an anxiety about becoming pigeonholed. But I won't say that the money on offer isn't a huge point of consideration. Sorry if that all sounds financially driven, but it's the truth and the reason that so many others are offering their services.

Sky has asked me to do some punditry work but I don't feel I'm at that stage of my career just now. The fee was £1,500, which certainly isn't to be sniffed at for an afternoon spent analysing a football match. A friend who has been on the circuit for a while told me that he is paid about £1,000 for a BBC pundit appearance and that he is chauffeured to and from his house, which is at the other end of the country. There is definitely a very good living to be made after football. I used to go on Soccer AM and feel guilty over the £800 fee because it was such a laugh. After the show, we'd go for beers at the crew's local and talk football. I have kept in contact with a few of them; it isn't the same today, but back then it was such a great show.

Years ago, if I said I played football, people would queue up to talk to me and buy me drinks no matter who I played for. Today if I go out to see friends I have to be on my toes. Everybody I meet seems to be a reporter. If you meet a footballer and he comes across as a rude, arrogant prick, the chances are that he is simply mimicking a Geoffrey Boycott innings – unspectacular without giving anything away too easily. Either that, or you have bumped into Ashley Cole.

Whatever the fallout of the Leveson inquiry, it won't stop some people from contacting the tabloids to tell them they have just seen a player come out of a hotel with a young lady who isn't his wife. I'd love to be more frank with the supporters who ask me how football really works, but I have been stitched up so many times that I think the only course of action is to take a vow of silence – this book excluded, of course.

CHAPTER 5
TACTICS

On the one hand, football is a very simple game. On the other, and out of the sight of prying eyes, it is one of the most intricate balancing acts in sport. In order for a team to be successful, at any level, there needs to be a perfect marriage between tactics, players and coaching. Years ago, I would have said that if a team had the best players they would always win, but today I can't deny the importance of astute management and tactical awareness.

Take Chelsea. Their 2011-12 season unravelled under the tactics and man-management style of André Villas-Boas, with the team losing their way in the Premier League and coming close to elimination from the Champions League. After a change of managers, they recovered in spectacular style, knocking out defending champions Barcelona en route to defeating Bayern Munich on their own patch in the final. Roberto di Matteo had exactly the same squad of players at his disposal but he used them more efficiently. Chelsea were less open and much harder to beat. Harmony was restored to the dressing room, with the reports of unrest drying up almost overnight.

These days, teams are so evenly matched at the very top level that a title can hang on a single decision by a manager. You might remember a dull game between Newcastle and Manchester City at St James'

Park towards the end of the 2011-12 season. City had to win this match if they were to stay ahead of Manchester United in the title race. With the game goalless and less than half an hour remaining, it was easy to imagine the blue half of Manchester screaming at the TV to get another striker on. Instead, City manager Roberto Mancini took off Samir Nasri, one of his most attacking players, and replaced him with Nigel de Jong, a holding midfielder. A few City fans must have been scratching their heads in wonder and even the commentators were a little perplexed at first. The substitution, however, allowed City to push Yaya Touré, who had previously been screening the back four, into a more attacking role. Less than 10 minutes later, De Jong passed to Touré, who was now 20 yards further up the pitch. He played a one-two on the edge of the box with Sergio Agüero, before angling a shot into the bottom corner of the Newcastle net. Twenty minutes later he scored again.

There is nothing lucky or accidental about good management. Having an intimate knowledge of each player is vital in today's game and, as the example above demonstrates, makes the difference between success and failure. When supporters and pundits alike were losing their heads in the heat of battle, Mancini kept his and City got the rewards.

I'm not saying that it always works. Indeed, it can backfire spectacularly, but being aware of the balance of the game at all times, coupled with knowing when it is right to deploy certain tactics, is a fundamental skill today. That may sound obvious, but circumstances do not always allow a manager to employ the strategies that he wants.

A manager once told me that in a match at Stamford Bridge between Chelsea and Manchester United, Alex Ferguson feared that his team were going to lose inside five minutes because of the way that Chelsea had set up to counter the threat of Cristiano Ronaldo. Apparently Ferguson was giving serious consideration to taking Ronaldo off as quickly as possible but decided against it because of how it would look, particularly so early in the game. That must have been an impossible situation. How could the club's star player, scoring almost every week and playing against United's biggest rivals at the time, be withdrawn with next to no time on the clock when he wasn't injured? Ronaldo's confidence and Ferguson's tactical reputation would both have been severely damaged, especially if United lost the game.

The level of detail that goes into games still amazes me. Every player has his own script: what to do, when to do it, information on the player he's up against, including weight, height, age, strengths, weaknesses, even what that opponent is likely to do when the ball comes to him in certain situations. We memorise every single set piece – where we have to stand, run and end up. We even memorise this for the other players, so we know where everyone else will be at any given time.

You know that pass when you say to yourself: "How did he spot that?" Often he didn't need to: he knew the player would be there because, the night before in the hotel, he read about the runs he would be making. It's exactly the same with the pass that leaves you saying: "Who was that to?" The receiving player either forgot to be there or was taken out of the game by a tactical manoeuvre by his opposite number. Football at this level is very chess-like, certainly to those inside the game. I sometimes wonder if it's more enjoyable playing lower down the leagues. After all, who wants to play chess?

With top-level football so complex, it is difficult to deconstruct a live game within a couple of minutes of it being over. Because of this, the "analysis" of these matches is usually reduced to goals and individual performance. But the fact that many pundits don't even try to scratch beneath the surface, despite knowing what it takes to win a match at this level, annoys me. It's a trivialisation of what we do by people who we used to call our own and, more importantly, it deprives the viewer of some interesting titbits that would, I feel, add to the entertainment.

Anyone can navigate a giant iPad, sliding the faces of famous players around with their finger while throwing out phrases like "third man run" and other such rubbish. What viewers really want is someone like Gary Neville, who has been a breath of fresh air on Sky. Neville, only recently retired, has offered genuine and relevant insight into matches, explaining *how* and *why* things happen, rather than just saying *what* happened. He's opinionated as well, in a way that isn't arrogant or designed to belittle the viewer, unlike Robbie Savage, who works on the basis that "I've played and you haven't, so if I shout louder, I win."

What particularly riles me is when you hear a pundit or co-commentator say something like: "Can't understand, Martin, why Drogba is not on the post here. That header would have fallen to him and if I'm Petr Cech I'm saying: 'Go on son – clear that off the line for me!'"

The fact is that corners are routinely cleared by a man stationed on the six-yard line, exactly where Chelsea would position Didier

Drogba. If somebody scores inside that post, it is for no other reason than a player having lost his man. Andriy Shevchenko's second goal for Ukraine against Sweden at Euro 2012 was a case in point. Mikael Lustig hardly covered himself in glory with the way he switched off on the goal line, but the goal would never have come about had Zlatan Ibrahimovich, who was standing on the corner of the six-yard box, beaten Shevchenko to the first header. Instead, he lost concentration and Shevchenko, with a clever run, nipped in front of him.

The point I'm trying to make is that if there is a player on the post he will clear possibly one or two shots or headers off the line a season. If that same player stands on the six-yard line he will probably clear 100 corners away over the course of the season. The worst thing, though, is when this dross gets into popular culture and my friends start saying stupid things to me like, "We should have a man on the post – our manager doesn't know what he's doing," just because it sounds like the right thing to say.

There are many more examples that are less obvious, but here the line between fact and fiction becomes a little hazy. The easiest way to create a scapegoat in the highlights is if a defender plays an attacker onside. For those who haven't realised, offside in the modern game is dead – it simply does not exist any more. Defences do catch attackers offside when it is obvious but no team, especially in the Premier League, spends any time in training practising how to catch players offside. The last team that I saw who tried to play the offside game in open play was Chelsea against Arsenal in 2011 under Villas-Boas. Chelsea lost as a direct result, after John Terry slipped near the halfway line after finding himself the last man. For my money, the man with the ball should never be the last man for exactly this reason. There are, however, certain situations when a defence needs to play the percentages where offside is concerned.

When a winger has the ball he will usually try to head for the byline to get his cross in, which naturally draws the defence deeper and deeper towards their own goal; but as soon as he comes back on his "opposite foot" (so he is now hitting an in-swinging cross), the defence will always step up and try to make the edge of the box because it is a sure-fire way of catching an attacker offside, as he is running in the opposite direction from the defence. When a winger cuts back, watch the defence – if they're well drilled they will all step up in unison. It also gives the goalkeeper the freedom of the penalty area to come and claim the cross without running into anybody. While on the subject of wingers checking back to deliver an in-swinging cross, this can leave attacking midfielders and strikers infuriated as they make their runs into the box expecting the first delivery but are forced, in effect, to make a double run because of the delay in crossing the ball.

Tactics are becoming more important as each club seeks to maximise its style of play and the resources at its disposal. During the past decade far more attention has been paid to the statistical analysis of football, which is why every Premier League club now employs a team of people to pore over the footage and data of their own players as well as those of their opponents.

The first time I came across any statistical analysis was when heart-rate monitors were introduced for training. The improvement in the technology means we can now take the ball down on our chest, rather than have it bouncing off in all directions. As with any new technology in football that directly involves the players, it was met with complete contempt by those of us who had to use the equipment. The overriding feeling at the outset was that the only reason we were using heart-rate monitors was to dig out players who weren't coming off the training pitch in need of an oxygen tank. It was the first example I experienced of the fads in football that hold us back by five or 10 years at a time.

Thankfully technology moves quickly and it wasn't long before Prozone came along to show us the benefits of data such as pass completions and entries into the final third, tracking player movements, distances between defenders, interceptions and turnover of play. In my view, certain elements of the Prozone system have highlighted attributes in some players that might otherwise have been overlooked, in particular defensive midfielders like Mikel John Obi, Wilson Palacios and Nigel de Jong. Don't forget – every interception made by these players is essentially the start of an attack for their own team.

I never cared too much for these statistics because I've always believed a player shouldn't need anyone to tell him whether he's played well or not. But when the numbers are pinned up in the changing room for everyone to see, it's impossible not to become competitive, which is obviously why they were put there in the first place. We had two players at one of my clubs who used to set out to outrun each other in matches and then eventually in training, for no discernible reason other than wanting to see their name in lights on the Prozone stats.

It's also worth remembering that these stats can be made available to everyone, so when we used to come up against teams where I'd been told that the manager "liked" me, I couldn't help but run a little further, try harder to win a few extra headers and make more tackles because it was another chance to impress. This scene was played out in a match against a Midlands club who I'd been told were keen to sign me. Unfortunately, I got knocked out early on and should definitely have gone off. Instead I carried on, against the physio's advice, and had one of my worst games ever. That put paid to any hope of that move coming off.

These days players do see the value of statistics in football, especially in pre-season, when the new vests that we wear, which cost about £15,000 each, enable our sports scientists to see in real time exactly how hard we're working. And that's not so much to pull anyone up for not trying hard enough; it's about injury prevention and stopping players from pulling muscles. Everyone is different and, because of the technology, clubs are now able to tailor programmes to each player, based on their physical ability. In other words, the days of players running up and down the stands or being sent off to an army camp to be "beasted" for a week are gone.

Recruitment is an area where statistics have become particularly influential in recent years, due in no small part to the Moneyball philosophy first used by the Oakland A's general manager, Billy Beane, in baseball. Soccernomics, the football equivalent, is the analysis of a set of numbers and player data used to give teams a competitive edge. It is not necessarily about finding great value in the transfer market; it's more a method of bringing players to the club who fit the tactical ethos of the manager and/or sporting director.

Damien Comolli, Liverpool's former director of football, employed a version of Soccernomics at Anfield, although it's questionable how much of a final say he had on what players were brought in during his time at the club. In an interview with France Football last year, Comolli said of Luis Suárez: "We turn enormously toward players who don't get injured. We also took into account the number of assists, his performances against the big teams, against the smaller clubs, in the European Cup and the difference between goals scored at home and away."

For most of us, those stats would be pretty obvious when signing a player. Perhaps a better example of Soccernomics at work would be the recruitment of Liverpool's left-back José Enrique, another Comolli signing underpinned by impressive data. When Liverpool failed in a bid for Gaël Clichy, it was reported that Comolli turned to Enrique after discovering that his statistical figures were far more impressive than Liverpool's scouting report suggested. He was also much cheaper than Clichy in terms of the transfer fee and salary. What stood out about Enrique, supposedly, was that he had one of the highest pass completions and entries into the final third; he could also be credited with having a direct hand in many of Newcastle's goals.

Stewart Downing's statistics in his final season at Villa were also highly impressive, although Liverpool fans will find that hard to believe after his first year at Anfield, when he scored no Premier League goals and finished without an assist to his name. I don't know what was going on behind the scenes at Liverpool but one thing that statistics will never show is the personal variables that accompany any move and can have a huge bearing on a player's success. We can all think of good players who have struggled to live up to their billing when they move to a new club.

When I made my own big-money move, the Prozone stats did not flag up the fact that my wife was perfectly happy where she was because she had all her friends and family around her, as well as a great job that she loved. I took it all away from her, which led to her becoming withdrawn and unhappy. I knew at the time that I was taking all of that baggage on to the pitch, as well as the pressure and responsibility of being relied upon to perform for a Premier League club.

In a Premier League where up to a dozen clubs are so closely matched in terms of players, many games are settled by set pieces or carefully choreographed training-ground routines in which meticulous preparation and statistical analysis can make the difference. In open play, a huge amount of study, from my own experience at clubs, is devoted to the calculation of what are described as final third entries, penalty box entries and regains of the ball in the final third (see Barcelona's "pressing game").

Stoke City's style is the most rudimentary example of Soccernomics on a football pitch. Each full-back generally looks for the striker Peter Crouch on an angle (final third entry) and, in turn, the forward will attempt to cushion the ball down into the penalty area (penalty box entry) for his partner or a midfield runner. It goes almost without saying that the higher these two statistics are over a season, the more likely Stoke are to end up with a shot on goal.

Add to that Rory Delap's long throws and the team's height, which they seek to exploit on set plays, and it is no surprise that Stoke score many of their goals in and around the six-yard box, where they have a succession of players making individually tailored runs. One tactic that they employ very well is the "block". The block is used for attacking free kicks and corners and involves a player literally step-ping across the path of a marker while his team-mate makes a free run either across the face of goal or "round the back", usually from a free kick. Most teams use a variation of the block and it is difficult to defend against, provided the ball hits the right area.

One of these variations came in the pivotal Manchester derby at Eastlands towards the end of the 2011-12 season, when Vincent Kompany headed the only goal of the game from a corner at the end of the first half. The key to the block isn't so much what's happening in the area but more the quality of delivery. Everybody can do their jobs in the box but if the ball doesn't land within two feet of where it is supposed to, the whole set piece will fail.

The ball, as is usually the case, was aimed "along the six-yard line". Somebody stands "on the keeper", so he can't easily collect it while the other players make their runs. Usually the attacking team will take their cue from one player who makes his run after a show of a hand from the corner-taker; this, in theory, means that everyone is working to the same timings thereafter. What was unusual about this set piece was that the ball was meant specifically for Kompany. Usually, as at Stoke, a host of players will attack it.

United would have realised that something choreographed was about to happen when Joleon Lescott stood facing away from the goal on the edge of the six-yard line level with the post, but obviously they wouldn't have had a clue where the ball would be delivered. Kompany started just inside the area and made a run towards Lescott. As soon as Kompany had moved his marker, Chris Smalling, close enough to Lescott, Kompany took two steps to the left, just enough to get that extra yard, while Lescott gave Smalling a gentle push to the right. The ball was perfect, along the "corridor of uncertainty", and City duly won the match.

Where the success of Soccernomics is concerned, Stoke are a great example of the match-up that is required between a set of tactics and the players who have the attributes to execute them to the fullest, while Manchester City are an example of a team that has world-class players who can pick out an individual rather than playing the percentages from every set piece.

A friend in the game told me that at Bolton Sam Allardyce studied hundreds of Premier League corners to see where the clearing header, on average, would land. Once he identified a pattern (it's usually a front-post header that is cleared towards the dugout), he placed a man on the exact spot where the ball generally made its first contact with the pitch; thus the odds of Bolton conceding a goal from the second phase of play were severely reduced.

Years ago, at my first club, the manager would spend hours coming up with set plays that he would go through with us on the training pitch. One role that is nearly always taken up at every level of the game is one I referred to earlier in the book, when I mentioned Charles Hughes and the "position of maximum opportunity" (Pomo). The Pomo is the space inhabited by a striker, usually after pulling away from the goalkeeper after a corner is taken. It is often defined as the space between the six-yard line and the back post and is important because a high percentage of headers won by the attacking team are flicked towards this area. God forbid if one of our forwards wasn't there. "That is the difference between you becoming a millionaire and spending the rest of your career at the fucking Dog and Duck!" the manager used to scream if someone went awol.

But football is not a matter of one pitcher trying to outfox one batter. It is a team game and no amount of statistics can allow for two players who can't stand to be in the same room as each other, no matter how many final-third entries they've made in the past two seasons. What's more, while we have transfer windows, "value" will always be a subjective term. Andy Carroll may have had amazing statistics but, with Liverpool's bank balance swollen from the sale of Fernando Torres to Chelsea, their being in desperate need of a striker and the transfer window closing, his price was always going to be skewed.

There are so many little things that a player can do to gain an advantage on the pitch. Whenever I would flick a throw down the line, I'd put my arm over the shoulder of the player behind me to stop him from jumping. I'd always win the header and the officials never saw it. From a free kick or corner into the box, I'd wait for my marker to look at the ball and then pull his arm towards me to throw him off balance; as soon as the defender was off balance he could never recover. That extra yard is everything in football, and that tactic was the only sure way that I found to lose my marker. I scored a good few goals from it, too. The beauty is that once you have done that to a defender, he will always give you an extra yard at the next corner for fear of being pulled off balance a second time.

Individual deceit is one thing but it will always be a collective effort that prevails, and today the evidence of that can be found in nearly every team in the country, as well as overseas. When I started playing football, the only teams who ever seemed to change their formation were Brazil and Holland. Holland would occasionally employ a sweeper system, while Brazil all but invented the wing-back.

As players have become more comfortable on the ball and faster with it, the need for two strikers has all but disappeared, certainly at the top level. Samuel Eto'o, when he played for Inter Milan, and David Villa at Barcelona have both been converted to what we used to know as the inside left and inside right positions, with one obvious result: crosses are coming from full backs (or not at all in the case of Barcelona) and conventional wing play is as dead as playing offside. In the modern game, everyone is trying to emulate Spain and, ultimately, Barcelona – five bordering on six midfielders who can play anywhere across the pitch, interacting with each other as quickly as possible. Tackling, as a means of winning the ball back, is slowly being replaced by a high-tempo, pressing game, where the emphasis is on regaining possession as high up the pitch and as quickly as possible.

How times have changed. In the early part of my career, the only comments you'd hear a manager shout were, "Let him know you're there early doors", "Win your tackles" and, slightly less violently, "If in doubt, kick it out". It's taken a long time but any fly on our dressing room wall today would hear, "Keep the ball", "Make sure of your passes" and, "Don't go to ground unless you have to". With the speed of the game, going to ground means a player is temporarily out of action, which can be the difference between being in the right place to prevent a goal or lining up to kick off again, having just conceded one.

One of the main problems for referees is that it's almost impossible to determine whether it is the intent of a player to win the ball or foul the man. That places everyone (players included) in an uncomfortable situation because one man's honest judgment is another's favouritism. The immediate solutions are limited but, in my opinion, the only answer is encouraging the next generation of players to abandon the tradition of tackling altogether and work harder on the real skills of the game. It's a shame so many of us, me included, enjoy going in for a tackle whether you win the ball or not.

One of the Premier League's most successful imports, Xabi Alonso, offered a damning explanation for why England can't crack it at international level. "I don't think tackling is a quality," said the Spaniard. "At Liverpool I used to read the matchday programme and you'd read an interview with a lad from the youth team. They'd ask: age, heroes, strong points, etc. He'd reply: 'Shooting and tackling.' I can't get into my head that football development would educate tackling as a quality, something to learn, to teach, a characteristic of your play. How can that be a way of seeing the game? I just don't understand football in those terms. Tackling is a [last] resort and you will need it, but it isn't a quality to aspire to, a definition."

He ended by touching on the biggest problem facing the next generation of England players. "It's hard to change because it's so rooted in the English football culture." During our games it is noticeable that every 50-50 challenge is met with a roar of approval from the crowd, and often there is a ripple of applause even if you don't win the ball. For some players, it is how they're accepted and how they judge whether they've had a good or bad game.

On one occasion I went sliding in to Dimitar Berbatov (I honestly thought I could win the ball) and afterwards the look on his face was one of total pity for me. He seemed saddened by the fact I had to resort to this, either because I wasn't as good as him or my football education was so flawed. Actually, I think it was both.

Last season Mancini asked for a red card for Liverpool's Martin Skrtel but also accused Wayne Rooney of doing the same for Kompany. In an interview after the Carling Cup semi-final, the City manager again asked why a red card was not shown to Liverpool's Glen Johnson before Steven Gerrard pointed out the Italian's double standards. I don't like seeing managers or players ask for red cards but I've been guilty of the same crime. I once asked the referee to send off John Terry but only succeeded in earning a yellow for him and a lot of abuse for me, mainly from the referee. I admit it's a cheap tactic that can make a player look bad. That said, I know that I feel a lot better when I win a match than when I lose one.

Everybody wants to be in a team that passes the ball but most players will be lucky to be in a position to have a choice. When a player starts their career, they're just happy to play but, over time, you become a bit more precious about what you want from the game. When a disgruntled player leaves a club, you'll often hear them say: "I just want regular first-team football." With some that will genuinely be the case but I also know dozens of players who have left clubs because they can't stand the tactics employed by the manager. That can then have a knock-on effect, whereby those players tell their mates in the game, word gets round and others are put off from signing for that club.

CHAPTER 6
THE BIG TIME

I am always being asked to name the best player I have ever played against. It is difficult to know how to answer. I have shared a pitch with Rooney, Henry, Ronaldo, Van Persie, Alonso, Drogba and Bale, to name a few. I even had a few of their shirts in an Ikea bag under my kitchen sink (more about that later). A little disrespectful, but storage in modern houses is at a premium, so take it up with David Wilson Homes.

None of these players has ever dazzled me in a match, probably because I was too busy chasing the ball to notice. But the first time I saw Paul Scholes was the first time that I really understood football and the importance of practice and of keeping yourself under the radar off the field to achieve a consistent level of performance. No wonder Barcelona's Xavi says Scholes is the best midfielder he has seen in the last 10 years. The interesting thing about this choice, however, is that Scholes was merely warming up before the match that we were about to play.

I had gone to chase a ball that had been hit into the stands and as I waited for the fans to do the thing that they find incredibly funny, namely holding on to the ball for as long as possible before throwing it back to the player with unnecessary force, I noticed Scholes clipping the ball back and forth with a team-mate. Eventually my ball came back. I signalled to my warm-up partner that I wanted to stretch and I went into a token groin lunge so I could take in the bulk of what turned out to be the most flawless display of passing and control I've ever seen. Both feet. Immaculate every time.

The most noticeable thing about playing in the Premier League, aside from the quality of players such as Scholes, is that there is absolutely no hiding place. Not from the fans, not from the officials and certainly not from the cameras. But before you can appreciate the big time, it is important to look back at where you have come from and how you got there. I spent some time at the beginning of my career developing my game in the lower leagues. It didn't bother me because at that time I was just happy to be playing a level of football that meant something more than a handful of people turning up to a reserve game. I didn't care that the Gay Meadow pitch had been under five feet of water the week before or that Sincil Bank was similar to playing on a sandy beach. It was first-team football.

Lower league opposition teams playing at a Premier League ground can sometimes find themselves overawed. I had that exact feeling the first time I played at Liverpool. The character and history were everywhere, from the moment I saw the "This is Anfield" sign to when I walked up the steps from the tunnel to the strains of You'll Never Walk Alone. That was the moment I felt football could not get any better – a thought that it is all too easy to get swept up in.

I held back from taking pictures and sending them to my friends, from touching that famous sign above the tunnel or looking up at the Kop just before the kick-off as the fans held their scarves aloft – there is such a thing as too much respect. I've learned two important things about playing against more illustrious opposition: never look across in the tunnel unless you know someone and never give the impression for one second that you don't belong there, even if the surroundings are a million miles away from what you are used to.

The contrast between clubs at the top and the bottom of the ladder is huge. At the lower-league club I played for, we had a kit man who resented giving you your kit each day because he had to wash it on his own, one physio who treated everything with ultrasound because that was the only machine he had, and a common that doubled as a training pitch. Most of my clubs since have included numerous kit men, physios, masseurs and fitness coaches working at a training ground with at least five practice pitches, full-time chefs and designated car parking. All of which reflects what football clubs can afford these days rather than what is actually needed.

And in football less can definitely mean more. I loved playing in games where the expectations were relatively low and nobody knew (or cared) who I was. There was a certain amount of freedom at that point in my career that is impossible to get back. I was able to build my confidence because people expected a kid to make mistakes as he learned his trade. Years later, the slightest miscontrol or wayward pass would understandably end with a bollocking. That puts pressure on a player to be impossibly perfect, which in my case has led to huge levels of frustration. I would love to be able to bring the innocence of my early playing days to my game today.

That said, the further down the football pyramid you go, the more obvious it is that for many players the game is a job that pays the bills. A lengthy injury at this level can be the difference between earning a new contract and finding a new occupation. At one club I played for, the captain appealed against a two-week fine on the grounds that he wouldn't be able to meet his mortgage repayment that month. As I recall, the fine was subsequently reduced to three days – one for each day that the manager felt his performance in training had suffered from going out on a night that infringed club policy.

That same pro, who had been at the club for years, once gave me advice on how to negotiate my contract. He had come up with his own system that seemed to work for him. "You don't want to ask for too much every time, because when a new manager comes in he might want to get you off the wage bill. You want to go up incrementally but never arrive at a point where a manager might think you are earning more than your worth; that way you'll always stay at the club and you'll always play." OK, he didn't use the word "incrementally" but that was the gist of what he was saying.

For me, it was crazy. Even as a young player, I wanted to earn as much money as I could because I knew that if I was picking up a fortune, that would mean I was playing for a big club in the Premier League. But that player was content at the club he was at; he was local(ish), he had kids in school nearby and his wife had a good job. Changing football clubs would probably have cost him money by the time he'd moved house and relocated his family. Imparting that kind of advice to a young player with a genuine chance in the game is a little misguided, although I understood what he was trying to say, even if he was 15 years too early.

In the Premier League there are no such concerns. Clubs can pay you a fortune even if you aren't playing, simply to keep you on the books as an asset rather than running the risk of you leaving on a free. And this is where you will find an interesting breed of footballer – the player who regularly changes clubs. Financially, there is a fortune to be made in the Premier League just by moving clubs, and it works like this: as long as a player doesn't officially ask to leave his current club, he is legally entitled to the remainder of the value of his contract (this is nullified if you hand in a transfer request).

The trick is to employ a very active agent while at the same time hiring a PR guru to keep your name in people's minds through carefully selected interviews and TV appearances. Take me. I wanted to leave a club that I had signed for because I wasn't playing. Because of this my transfer value was falling and the club were desperate to realise an ever-depreciating asset. The sticking point was that I was earning £1.4m a year and had about twelve months left on my current deal. We entered into negotiations in which I told them how happy I was at the club and how I didn't want to leave. Eventually we settled on a severance fee of more than £500,000 to be paid quarterly over the following year. Now that sounds like a lot of money – probably because it is – but it saved the club from paying out more than double that sum in wages while also securing them a transfer fee on a player who was never going to play. Good business all round.

And after leaving the club, I was able to name my price at the other end. I had earned around £30,000 a week at the club I had left and so the club that wanted to sign me were going to have to get as close to this as possible, which they did. And, typically, a player can expect a signing-on fee of roughly 10% of the transfer fee (in truth it is whatever you can negotiate). This was the only time I found myself in this situation, because I prefer to stay in one place for as long as I can, but there is a fortune to be made by settling up your contract and taking a signing-on fee at the other end.

Imagine if you were to do this every year. You could easily trump a player at a top-four team who has been there for 10 years, earning £70,000 a week. Now think of some of the players who have constantly been on the move in their careers, and the size of the transfer fees – Robbie Keane stands out, as do Nicolas Anelka and Craig Bellamy. Each time these guys move, they settle a portion of their contract and take a huge signing-on fee, as well as a large basic wage.

This also happens in the lower leagues, where managers tend to be a lot more hands-on with the finances. There is a very well-known story about a manager at one club who was trying to get rid of his captain. He called him into the office and asked him point-blank how much it would take to pay him off. The player replied, "25k", at which point the manager produced a cheque from his desk drawer made out to the captain for this exact amount. The manager who told me the story said that he had pre-written cheques ranging from £10,000 to £50,000 because he wasn't entirely sure what the player was going to ask for. What he was sure about was that the player was going to be leaving his club that day.

At the top level, bonuses become incredibly important. I have lost count of the horror stories I have heard about squads of players who have made it all the way through to a final, snuck into Europe and even won promotion, only to realise that there was never an agreed bonus. But trying to get a squad of 30 players to agree on bonuses is the stuff of nightmares; it is the one time when I do not envy the captain. Why players don't club together to pay a top agent or lawyer to draft something for them is beyond me.

To give you an example of bonuses, I have dug out a contract from one of my first seasons in the Premier League. At this club, the bonuses were paid on a per point basis, depending on league position as follows:

1st to 3rd: £2,500 a point
4th to 6th: £1,500 a point
7th to 12th: £1,000 per point
13th to 20th: nothing

We also had a bonus for finishing in a certain league position, with the pot split between the playing squad. This, in turn, was based on games played. Each position in the table was reflected in a payment from the Premier League, prize money generally going up by a significant six-figure sum for each position on the ladder. Add in the millions that come in from TV rights for another year in the Premier League and it's easy to see why we tried to negotiate a piece of all of it. Our pot was usually around £2m, of which I'd take home somewhere between £50,000 and £70,000.

Bonuses for cup competitions were always poor as the club used to field their reserve side, mainly because they were preoccupied with the Premier League. For example, for winning the Carling Cup, the matchday squad would split a pot of £25,000 while the FA Cup was a little better, at £100,000 across the squad. At the top clubs that figure would be per man.

At some clubs I played at we even used to have bonuses based on the size of the crowd – 12,000 to 20,000 was £500 and anything over 20,000 spectators was £1,000. This was because the club knew full well that nobody would come to the cup games. In truth, everything is up for negotiation. I've had bonuses that rewarded playing consecutive games (an incentive not to get injured), scoring goals or winning a certain number of games, as well as clean sheet bonuses and even bonuses for being called up internationally. I've had lump sums paid to me for every 10 games played, and bonuses on top of bonuses.

But these things can sometimes work against you. It's all very well having the bonuses but if you fall out of favour on a heavily incentivised contract, it might turn out to be the worst decision you ever made. So many players that I know have not been able to play once they reach a certain number of games for a club because once they play one more match to hit a specific figure, either a payment must be made to the player's previous club or a clause is triggered wherein the player gets a pay rise and an extended contract.

Seth Johnson found himself in this position at Leeds, where he ended up stuck on 59 appearances because another match would have triggered a £250,000 payment to Derby County, his previous club. It still happens today. You might not have any sympathy. After all, the player is still earning a healthy wage. But that isn't the point. It's extremely frustrating when you're fit and desperate to play but prevented from doing so because of a contract clause that the club were happy to agree to at the time. It's like being blindfolded while two supermodels tear each other's clothes off in front of you.

When a Premier League club that I played for wanted to sell me, they had to pay my previous club a sell-on fee of 10%. This is quite standard. The previous club will usually have certain add-ons in the event of a player going on to great things, such as playing for his country or playing over 100 games for his new club. My previous club were in line for hundreds of thousands of pounds if the sale went through and, with money being tight, it was a chunk of change that I know they would have welcomed.

I say "would have" because the club I was at approached my old club and told them that unless they took £50,000 they would refuse to sell me and the club would end up with nothing. There was little, if anything, that my old club could do. They took the £50,000. But before you feel sorry for them, this had a knock-on effect. Somebody at the smaller club will at some point have had a similar conversation with his counterpart at an even smaller club. During this time, I was being told that the sale wouldn't go through because my previous club were refusing to budge, and would I mind having a word with them?

This was highly inappropriate but quite clever on the part of the club I was with. If I'd made that call, I would have lost any right to a severance payment because effectively I would have admitted that I wanted to leave. As soon as I did that, any claim I had to the remainder of my contract would have been null and void.

The Premier League is at the top of this food chain: it has its own TV deal, its own governing body and even its own rules. It plays the tune that the rest of British football is forced to dance to. Not that anyone getting a slice of the cake will complain.

Other than the money, one of the main things that stands out in the Premier League, especially at the top clubs, is that a lot of the players are built like cruiser-weights. They are solid, the tackles feel stronger and the tussles are that much harder to win. (Antonio Valencia once blocked a clearance of mine and I swear it was like being hit by a car. That's what I remember thinking as several fans helped me out of the stand and back on the pitch.)

Even if a player isn't overly quick in a flat race he will certainly be sharp when it comes to what is known as the "five-yard frenzy". Each player has a radius of five yards where he will try his hardest, run as fast as he can, harry the player on the ball and generally try to win the ball back. Then the next player along will do the same until eventually possession is regained. Different teams employ different variations of this. You will see Barcelona do this as far up the pitch as they possibly can, so as to win the ball back close to the opposition goal. Stoke City, on the other hand, employ the method as soon as a team enters their half of the pitch with the ball.

In the lower leagues you can generally move past a player even in this five-yard radius but at the top it is nearly always better to pass and move if you're a mere mortal. This shows how good Xavi, Messi, Iniesta and Ronaldo are – to be able to glide through half a team of world-class players, each employing this method, is nothing short of astonishing.

The game is slower at the top than in the lower leagues, but there is more emphasis on sporadic bursts of play rather than sustained pressure. If you pick the ball up in front of your back four you could while away an afternoon quite happily passing it about between your full-backs and wide men, occasionally bouncing it off an advanced midfielder or centre-half. As soon as the ball is played goal-side of the defending team's midfield, that is when all hell breaks loose. It is so fast that, sometimes, even if you're standing in the right place, the ball moves too quickly for you to do anything about it. The speed at which players like Ronaldo manipulate the ball can be daunting.

One-touch football around the box is the biggest danger to defences in the Premier League. It gives you no chance to manoeuvre yourself into a position to deal with it. Luckily it is extremely difficult to execute because it has to be done incredibly accurately and at speed, and that has never been an easy combination.

Yet there are some aspects off the field where the Premier League is still catching up. Changing rooms can be poor, for example, where grounds date back to a different era. Interestingly, though, even here the home side's dressing rooms frequently have all of life's luxuries – unlike the visitors'. The latter will have suffered years of abuse as team after team has traipsed back in from the pitch after being on the receiving end of a hiding.

Many of these changing rooms, such as White Hart Lane, Old Trafford and Anfield, haven't changed much in decades, and just in my time playing the game I have seen a huge amount of vandalism in each of them. The more teams you play for, the more often a player will share a story with you, along the lines of: "Yeah, you see where those tiles used to be? That was where our goalkeeper lost his head and started punching the wall after we lost last year." Then there are the tell-tale signs of a squiggly mass of mastic on the wall by the sinks: this is not a labourer's attempt to replicate a Jackson Pollock, but simply where a mirror used to reside. "Yeah, our gaffer smashed that after we lost in the last minute." I suppose it adds to the character, but it's still vandalism. Not that I am a saint. If you go to Fratton Park you'll see an enormous dent in the side of one of the baths. We all lose our heads occasionally.

I have never particularly cared where I got changed. I have changed (and warmed up) on team buses when we have been late for games, and I have changed in prefabs and outhouses. On one occasion I had to get stripped in front of the crowd after the ceiling of our changing room fell in under the weight of water that hadn't drained away. Not once has it made a blind bit of difference to me.

Many of these stadiums look a lot better on TV than they do in real life. A row of fantastic corporate facilities often hides an uncomfortable truth. Many of the older stadiums, such as Leeds United's Elland Road, are in some places literally falling apart. And pitches that look great on TV are different again in the flesh. The first time I played at St James' Park (Newcastle, not Exeter), I couldn't believe the slope in one corner. It was the same at Nottingham Forest's City Ground. Not that I care. It doesn't make a blind bit of difference. It is actually a comfort to see that not everything is perfect all of the time.

But nothing can prepare you for forty, fifty, sixty or seventy thousand fans who have completely lost their heads after a goal. There aren't many places where one can experience such a release of positive emotion en masse. That's what I love about football: for a split second, tens of thousands of people could not be happier. And if you are the person responsible for that, you have every right to walk off the pitch feeling 10ft tall. I can feel the hairs on my neck standing up as I type that, because I know what it's like.

The adrenaline can take over at times. It then manifests itself, depending on what type of person you are, in a bad tackle, baiting an opponent or going too far with the ref. As great a player as Scholes is, some of his tackles are truly shocking and he's normally good for at least one every season. But then again, they do say to watch out for the quiet ones.

At this level, though, the game is moving so fast that it is very difficult to keep up with everything that's going on. This is when referees are grateful for a little help. During one match, I and another player had a running battle that started with mouthing off, then a couple of bone-crunching tackles and carefully positioned elbows, followed by downright vindictiveness such as pinching and hair-pulling (yes, honestly). The third time that the referee pulled us up, he simply said: "Look, if neither of you is going to knock this shit on the head, then at least don't let me catch you doing it." You can't argue with that.

Occasionally, however, referees get rather too much help. In Chelsea matches, Terry might as well have a whistle, such is his influence on decisions. The man gets away with murder on the football pitch. From one ball towards the box he caught me with a horrendous elbow that he should have been sent off for – but, standing over the referee with a carefully positioned hand on the shoulder, he got away with it. Later in the game, I matched myself up with him from a free kick and, as it was taken, I kicked him as hard as I could across the back of his legs and he crumpled to the ground. He went off for treatment but I was convinced this was nothing more than a ploy to draw attention to the fact that the referee had missed something, and that this something was carried out by me. He re-entered the pitch shouting something or other in my direction (I wish I could remember what it was) but I simply looked at him and said: "Come near me again, mate, and you'll get another one." As it turned out, there was only one more occasion in the second half when the ball dropped right between us and neither of us went in for it full-blooded. I guess you could say that deep down we're both shithouses.

To be honest, this sort of thing goes on all the time, at all levels. After the game I always make a point of seeking out my opponent to shake his hand, not because I am a gentleman (even I wouldn't try to get away with that) but because if he does not reciprocate, then I know that it has affected him and the next time we play that may be the difference between winning and losing. To date, not one player with whom I have had a run-in has refused to shake my hand.

The effort that goes into winning a game at this level is incredible. I take just as much pleasure from beating a newly promoted team as I do from beating a top team. It is another victory in the Premier League and it takes huge collective effort to pull it off. And that is what makes losing a match so hard to take. It is often said that a team in form fears nobody, and a run of games such as Fulham at home, Wigan away and Aston Villa at home looks like nine points before a ball is even kicked. But look at the same sequence of fixtures after a run of seven or eight games without a win and suddenly the same matches all start to look tricky.

If you lose to a team that you know will be at the bottom it is doubly hard to take, because more often than not the next fixture will be against a team that is closer to the top. It doesn't take an awful lot for a bit of panic to set in around a football club. Three defeats on the bounce and everyone is suddenly under pressure. This is why I often say that at the top level, more than any other, the enjoyment is negated by expectation and hard facts. Get relegated and not only does your reputation suffer but, more importantly, friends lose their jobs.

I'd be lying if I said that I didn't enjoy watching myself on Match if the Day. It's especially exciting if you have scored, because you can see everything that you missed at the time: the fans going nuts; the manager running from his dugout pointing both index fingers at his temples while looking at his defence; the other players hugging each other and the despair on the opposition's faces (I love seeing that last one). I know it sounds strange to say that you need to watch the game again to appreciate the supporters' celebrations after scoring but, generally, you quickly find yourself surrounded by seven or eight players, patting you and pushing your head down – a gesture of affection in football – so all you see is boots and the turf. By the time your team-mates disperse and you have a chance to lift your head and bask in a moment of personal glory, the supporters' attention has moved from you, the goal-scorer, to baiting the opposition.

I have come to realise, however, that much of what is shown in the Premier League highlights has been manipulated to fit a narrative that has two basic requirements: a hero and a villain. These could be anybody: a player, a manager, the referee, one of his assistants. The top teams generally have heroes, while the bottom teams get villains because this is the easiest sell. The easiest way to spot a narrative will be to watch a newly promoted team who create a shedload of chances, don't score and get beaten 2-0 by Chelsea. The narrative will either be that Petr Cech has had a great game, the newly promoted striker is not cut out for this level or top players like Drogba are the difference and always will be "at this level".

In a newly promoted side that I played in, I remember losing a match in what was a poor game. We had two chances: the first was a header from a free kick that the goalkeeper saved; the second was a one-on-one that was chipped on to the roof of the net. Both were offside and both were given as free kicks to the opposition. On Match of the Day, however, both were portrayed as missed chances by our striker. In the first clip, you could clearly see the assistant referee's flag go up at the top of the screen, and in the second clip you could hear the referee's whistle before our striker had even shot. The goalkeeper, as I recall, had even stopped to applaud his defence for catching the striker offside. I know it doesn't sound like a lot, but that sort of thing really pisses me off. Down the other end, a seasoned striker scored a header that was held up on TV as an example of how clinical you need to be. At this level, of course.

Away from the pitch, the kudos of being a Premier League footballer is evident everywhere that you go; everyone wants to be associated with it. Indeed, it always seems strange to me that the higher you go in football and the more you earn, the more you are actually given for free. When I started playing, we used to have a gold

McDonald's card that allowed the holder to walk in to any "restaurant" and order a free meal once a day. Today we are inundated with sports drinks, chewing gum, under-armour (the tight-fitting clothing that aids your performance and recovery) and grooming products. When one of our players has a baby, you can't move at the training ground for Harrods hampers and baby clothes. Car dealers are queueing up to lease cars at ridiculous prices, while tailors, mobile phone companies, security firms and property companies are desperate to make appointments through the club secretary simply to get in front of the players and offer their services.

Very often the cost is negligible in return for an endorsement on the company website. My mobile phone bill, for example, is a flat £20 per month and I call people all over the world, surf the internet and text as if it's about to go out of fashion. All I have to do is agree to a quote like: "[Company X] are a team of extremely hard-working, dedicated and friendly professionals. I couldn't be happier with the service." Nauseating, isn't it? Where Company X probably makes its money, in addition to the business that comes in on the back of footballers' names, is in supplying players with personal phone numbers, which usually feature their squad numbers several times over.

The higher a player goes, the more obscene it becomes. A friend of mine who was playing for England at the time told me that a property company working on the Palm project in Dubai approached David Beckham with an offer of a villa in return for an endorsement. My friend said that Beckham agreed, on condition that every other member of the squad was offered a villa at cost price – about £600,000. Today those villas are worth between £3m and £7m. So far as I know Trevor Sinclair actually lives in his now. Right place, right time. Good luck to him.

But I'm not a total sell-out. I've turned down stupid money when I've found a pair of boots that are really comfortable, even if that company isn't interested in sponsoring me. Nike have this market sewn up – a slicker operation you could not wish to see. Each season they go around each club with the most beautiful black pick-up truck, custom-made and with every size of new-model boot in the back. They park it right next to the youth team training pitch, and when the kids have finished training they simply hoover up the salivating egos of these impressionable youngsters. In theory that should be them, hooked, for the rest of their careers. Adidas went the other way and chose to target the top three players at the top six clubs in each league across Europe. Unfortunately for the German manufacturer, Nike had already hoovered most of them up too.

There is a flip side to the fame, however. There is a difference between what some players actually want and what is offered to them free of charge. I found this out first-hand at our last Christmas party. We had booked a table at a nightclub in Chelsea that, apparently, was the latest place to be seen. I don't really keep up with any of that: so long as there is a friendly crowd, decent music and a few bottles of chilled Corona I'm more than happy.

Outside the club, the queue was horrendous and, being that time of year, it was freezing cold. One of the players knew somebody who worked there; he went to the main entrance and asked to talk to his contact, but he wasn't in. My friend explained the situation, and at first the doormen seemed sympathetic, but there is always some power-crazed idiot who has to pipe up. Every top nightclub in London these days seems to employ a drop-dead gorgeous woman with legs up to her armpits, whose sole job is holding a clipboard. As much as we tried, she was not having any of it.

She was insisting on a minimum spend. As soon as my friend told her that we had booked under the name of the football club, she smelled money. She began by saying that we should have been there earlier and that she'd had to let the table go; she might be able to put us down for the next table but she'd have to insist that the minimum spend was £7,000. This was about £300 each, which, without being arrogant, was neither here nor there for us. But, out of principle, we stuck together and refused to part with a penny. They didn't let us in and it turned out to be the worst Christmas party in living memory, but I was proud of the boys nonetheless.

I learned a huge amount from spending time lower down the ranks. First and foremost – and this isn't meant with any disrespect – it gave me the motivation that I needed never to go back, at least not as a player. I gained a huge amount from seeing a couple of bitter thirty-somethings going about complaining that the big money in the game had never found its way into their pockets, while scolding anybody who dared to dream of bigger and better things. I have probably had far too much pampering for my own good but at least the two players at my first club toughened me up and ensured that, to some degree, I kept my feet close to the ground. Sometimes I wonder what became of them. Most of the time, however, I wonder what became of me.

CHAPTER 7
AGENTS

Players have become so valuable in the last 10 years that some agencies have stooped to incredible lows to secure their signatures. The transfer of Wayne Rooney to Manchester United saw legal action as one agency wrestled the player away from another.

The days of brown envelopes at the top level are in decline but it still happens. I had dinner with a chairman of one club not long ago. He told me that his manager would risk it all for £500 in cash – not because he needed the money but because he could. My friend turned a blind eye to it because the manager was so successful at the club and so well respected.

I won't deny that there are plenty of sharks out there and that some very underhand things go on. I won't defend this on the grounds that it is the same in any other industry, because that doesn't make it right. But away from the headlines and the myths are some very professional, very credible and very sharp people who have made a lot of players, including me, a lot of money over the years.

It is fair to say that agents get a bad press. They are an easy mark for football-obsessed media that are convinced that the public appetite is for negative stories about what they do and how they do it. The problem is that agents are the one part of football that the media truly don't understand and, in turn, the reports and programmes are consumed by an audience who know even less.

The sort of crap churned out by Channel 4's Dispatches and the BBC's Panorama only reflects the interests of people who probably don't have a passion for football, have certainly never kicked a football, have no clue as to how transfers happen and couldn't tell you what teams made up the Premier League before they were given the job by the commissioning editor.

The investigative media tend to go through fads where football is concerned. First we had the Fifa bung scandal, right before England attempted to win the vote to host the 2018 World Cup finals, then the racism reports ahead of Euro 2012. Both are subjects that fully deserve investigation, but the reports were put together poorly by people with tenuous links to the football world. The nadir was Channel 4's Dispatches programme on drugs in football, which spent an hour trying to get to the bottom of a problem that barely exists.

Documentaries about agents seem to be a constant trend across all channels that have an interest in football. In all of these exposés, there will be an interview with an "agent". They don't say precisely what the agent does but he is an agent nonetheless. He is always filmed so that you can't see his face, and very often his voice has been modified (I know the feeling). And, as you listen, you get a sense that this person hasn't been involved in the game for nearly 10 years and has no clue about how things are done today at the top level.

The only way to get a genuine insight is to read the thoughts of a real football agent who knows the industry inside and out. So rather than digging out someone who operated before the Premier League was even established, I've asked one of the most respected and influential agents in the game, who has brokered some of the biggest deals in world football, to answer questions from my followers on Twitter. He must remain anonymous.

@ Wdtarrant: "How do footballers choose their agent? Are they randomly approached? Recommended?"

Agent: "All of my existing clients came to me by way of recommendation but very often an agent acting alone or as part of a large agency firm will think nothing of cold calling, usually with an opening line of, 'I've got a club for you.' Agents who are new to the game and getting themselves established will either strike it lucky with one player who started out as a friend and has gone on to bigger and better things; or, more likely, an agent, if he is not already affiliated to one of the big six agencies, will make a series of random approaches to youth-team players after academy matches. They will literally loiter outside the changing rooms, waiting for the kids to come out. It's crude and it doesn't work with the top pros but you'd be amazed how many kids can be won over with a free pair of boots. As a result lots of clubs have stopped agents attending academy matches. If a player is under 16 he is legally not allowed to have an agent. Between the ages of 16 and 18, he can sign with an agent under parental consent.

"The point that follows is that the biggest agencies get a large number of players. There are six main agencies that represent nearly all the players and they want to be able to say to a prospective client that they represent 600 footballers. They almost operate a franchise where 80 agents have access to the same building. So if I'm affiliated to one of these super-agencies and I want to impress a potential client, then I will invite him to my huge offices in London with the glass frontage and a stable of agents split across 20 storeys and the player thinks to himself, 'This guy is really successful.' But he's not. He's just part of a franchise."

@Horrox93: "To what extent is an agent responsible for initiating a transfer? Or is it down almost entirely to the two clubs involved?"
Agent: "Answering the second part first, only occasionally and when there is an existing relationship. If one of my players is doing well, then he will want to move up but his club won't want to sell him. If he's doing badly, then the club will want to sell him but he may want to sit on his current contract if he knows that the deal he has will not be waiting for him elsewhere. So then you are into compensation packages. All of these scenarios need an agent who can work in the best interests of the club or the player because neither can do everything themselves.

"Very often the club will employ its preferred agent to go after a target. Let's say that a club wants a new left back and at the top of their list is Ashley Cole. The club will give the agent information such as how much they want to spend on a transfer fee, how much they are prepared to spend in wages and how long they are prepared to sign him for. The agent then goes into the market and finds out if that player is available and if he would be interested in signing. This is otherwise known as 'tapping up'.

"Usually the first choice is either too expensive or does not want to leave his current club, and so it is my job to work down the list. A club may then sign its second choice and in the press conference they'll say that they have been watching the player for a long time and he was their number one target, but we all know he wasn't."

@*Simonxthomas: "Are agents' fees for transfers reasonable or excessive?"*
"Five per cent is reasonable – at least that's what the FA say is reasonable. It is usually based on the guaranteed salary package for the player, but that is not set in stone and there are many ways of working the deal. A huge number of deals are well over 5%. Are the top agencies excessive? Yes, probably, but then there is no regulation to prevent the agency asking for as much as they like. For example, if a club tells me that it has £10m to spend on new players, does that mean for everything or just transfer fees? It is the same for agencies. Fifa want an agent's fee to be 3% but they won't say where that 3% should be coming from. Is it the transfer fee? Is it the salary package? Three per cent of what?

"One of the biggest reasons the Premier League experienced its first boom of foreign players was that agents, managers, chairmen etc suddenly realised that those players did not understand the market and their value within it. Today most of Europe has wised up but that situation is being repeated now with a lot of the African players who are coming in to the Premier League.

"When the time comes to sell the player, providing he's done well, then the agency will work for the club because the payday will be bigger. If one of those African players moves on for £20m, the agent may earn up to 20% of the selling price.

"I recently took a player from the lower leagues into the Championship. I have looked after this player as a favour to a friend for a couple of years and I would have looked after him for free because the fees for agents in the lower leagues are neither here nor there. As it turned out, he had a great season and was coveted by two-thirds of the Championship and one or two Premier League clubs. We decided that, as he is still young, it didn't make any sense to be on the bench at a big team, and he wanted to play in any case. In the end, we went to a biggish Championship side that offered him first-team football and a chance to continue his education. The club is also known as a selling club, so if he does well he'll almost certainly be sold on again at a time when he is ready to make the jump up in quality.

"But the point is that I have invested my time and money in this player for no guaranteed return. He would never have had the opportunity to earn the amount of money that he is earning now without an agent because clubs would have seen him coming a mile off. He has no idea what the going rate is, or indeed what he is worth in terms of wages. He doesn't know what Championship clubs pay; he isn't aware of all the intricacies that a transfer involves; he doesn't know that some Championship clubs pay more than some Premier League clubs; he doesn't know what sort of bonuses are paid; he wouldn't have known to ask for a sell-on fee and loyalty bonus, never mind how much to ask for. It's too much to take in for a player. When people ask me why players don't do their own deals, it's all I can do not to laugh. Players have no idea what each club is paying in terms of wages and they have no contacts at these clubs to engineer a move if they are not happy where they are. Players need to concentrate on playing – that's it. They are not financial experts or market experts. They would be taken to the cleaners.

"Now that this player is achieving a level of success, it is right and proper that the people who put him there are rewarded for their help and expertise. The selling club needs to be rewarded for taking a chance on the player with a transfer fee, the player needs to be rewarded for a great season with a good wage, and the agent needs to be rewarded with a fee for investing his time, effort and resources in the player. I will take a player from the lower league to the top. I have placed the player at the club and he has done well; I found a buyer and got him the move. I should be rewarded because there is a hell of a lot of work in among all that.

@FootballAway: *"Do you have a favourite club, and have you ever been tempted to guide a player towards (or even away from) your own child-hood club?"*

"It's an easy question. I do have a favourite club but I can honestly say that it has never impacted on any of my players' decisions. If it's a choice between moving one of my players to Manchester United, which might be my club, or Manchester City, we will choose the club that the player wants to go to and where the best deal is. In truth, I don't think it has an impact on any agency. If I'm appointed by a club to find them a left back who must have played in the Premier League, then I will try my hardest to find the best player within their budget. If that player happens to play for the club I support and he also happens to be our best player, it won't make one bit of difference.

@TristanCarlyle: *"How would football change if no agents were involved in player transfers? Which high-profile moves would never have happened?"*

"It's impossible to answer the last part of that question but the role of agents is to bring parties together around the table. It is very difficult without an intermediary to bring two clubs and a player to the same room at the same time. No matter how much they want to do the deal, somebody has to take the lead and organise each of them.

"So far as transfers that would never have happened are concerned, nearly all foreign transfers would have been very difficult to do in the early days, because the foreign agents did not have the market knowledge required to do business here in the UK. You might think that football is football but there is so much to consider when taking a player into a different country. Very often the way the players are paid is completely different. There may be more TV money available in one league than another; the club may have a vice-president who does the deals rather than a director of football; image rights may be appropriate. These nuances require a market expert, just as I am a market expert in the UK. To navigate this dilemma, agents will very often join forces with their counterparts in that country.

"When the Premier League exploded, foreign agents had no idea how much to ask for in salary for their players, or what they could expect by way of a fee. In the early days, many of them and their clients were vulnerable. Without UK-based agents opening the door, the foreign players would not have landed in this country for another 10 years and neither would the foreign managers, scouts, sports scientists, nutritionists and coaches or, almost certainly, the foreign owners. The moment the Premier League became global through the huge worldwide television audiences, it became a much more attractive investment for foreign owners. That could not have happened without agents opening these doors. But make no mistake: we did it for the money.

"Where would we be now? We'd be back to the bad old days. If you look around any changing room, the chances are you are going to see a few players where you think to yourself: 'How did you find your way to training today?' Now imagine how the owners used to exploit the gulf in understanding 20 years ago, even 10 years ago. That leads to disgruntled employees, poor performance and unhappy fans. The obvious question to ask would be: 'If agents are really so bad, why does every player, every manager and coach and every club use them?'"

@Nikhalton: "When a player and a club want a contract renewal, what do you do and what do you get paid for this?"
"Every case is different. For example, a contract renewal for an 18-year-old is restricted because he can't leave the club for free if the club he is currently at offers him more money. Nearly every club will do this regardless of whether they want to keep the player or not, because they stand to receive a compensation package set by a tribunal if they get wind that another club are interested in his signature. This applies to any player up to 24 years of age and there are various tiers of compensation for players who are in the academy or foreign and so on.

"But if a player has six months left before being a Bosman, then it's a different negotiation again because once you are 24, then the chances are you have played a good percentage of games, done well and, as a result, have a market value. Look at Robin van Persie. There comes a point where paying a premium for a contract renewal is the best option, because the club stands to lose the player for nothing and even if it decides to sell there are only two windows left, where the offers will be take-it-or-leave-it. In this situation, it would not be uncommon for an agent to pick up a sizeable fee because in the grand scheme of things Van Persie will score the goals that net Arsenal £30m in Champions League revenue. Then there's the cost of having to replace him, the feelgood factor that his signature will generate at the club and the message that his signing sends to other players that the club covets. It says: 'This is a good club; why look anywhere else?' That is important to players who are choosing which top club to sign for.

"Fees received vary, depending on the individual circumstances of the player. It depends so much on the value of the player. As I say, if it's an 18-year-old kid, it could well be nothing. If it's a top player, then there will be a premium attached to him."

@Davidhigman: "How do you feel about accusations that agents are ruining the game?"

"I would say that this continuing question comes from a lack of knowledge of the industry, ill-informed media and a general lack of understanding of how football really works. If something goes wrong, it's easy to blame a faceless agent. If a manager messes up with a player or vice versa, then there still has to be a very public continuing working relationship; all of that means that the best option is to blame the agent.

"The Wayne Rooney situation last season is a perfect case in point. The agent used the new wealth of Manchester City to get his client the best possible deal at Manchester United. You use one club to open the door at another – that's a standard practice. There is nothing wrong with that. Once Rooney got his contract at United, Fergie couldn't blame Rooney as he had the previous week, and so he hanged the agent in public, allowing for a working relationship with the player to continue. It happens at every club; Rooney's case got a lot of attention because he was the most high-profile.

"I wouldn't say agents are ruining football at all. Teams are getting their players, players are getting their wages and the fans are getting great entertainment. The deals go ahead but the way they go ahead varies dramatically, depending on the moral compass of the agent.

"Look at it another way – look at the product we are providing here and look at the most common complaints from the fans. Usually I hear, 'I pay £30 for my ticket.' Yes, you do but Sky are putting the money in now, not you. Football could survive without a single person going to the match. Then it's usually followed by, 'Why is that player getting £50,000 a week?' Easy, because Sky have just bought the TV rights for over £1bn. The recently agreed rights package for three years commencing 2013-14 has increased by over 70% for domestic TV rights, with the figure now at an astronomical £3.018bn. Even the team finishing bottom of the Premier League in that first season will earn more than £60m – that's the same figure that Manchester City received for winning the title in 2011-12. If you don't like hearing that and you want to blame somebody, then rather than pointing the finger at the agent, point it at the chief exec, point it at the chairman, point it at Sky or yourself. Everybody is winning in the Premier League. You can stay at home and watch the game live on TV, or you can go down the pub and watch it on a Greek decoder. The money is there, the product is there; everybody is winning."

@Jaykelly83: "Why don't more players use the service provided by the Professional Footballers' Association for contract renewals instead of an agent? Or, failing that, a solicitor?"

"A major problem with the PFA acting for a player is that it is perceived that they can't upset the clubs in a way that might be beneficial for their client. And while that is the case, representation by the PFA – who, let's not forget it, are the union – will always be a complete and utter conflict of interest. The perceived view in football where PFA representation is concerned is that the middle ground, where deals are won and lost, always tends to favour the club. If you knew that, would you want them representing you? Hardly any senior players use the PFA to negotiate their deals for this reason. Outside of the rules, agents that talk to clubs get the best deals for their players. Tapping up happens every day of the week; anyone who doesn't admit to that is lying.

"Solicitors are becoming involved on very specific points where contracts are concerned and an agent will outsource certain parts of a contract, like image rights, to a specialist. It won't surprise anybody to hear that a lot of solicitors are trying to enter the agency world because they will earn more money charging a percentage of a deal than they will if they charge by the hour. The problem they face is that there is no substitute for market knowledge and, as of now, most solicitors simply do not have that expertise.

"For example, I represent a player who has played in a small league abroad that has within it some huge grudge games, which are watched by tens of thousands of fans and are as big as any derby over here. The player had no reputation in England but he asked if I could represent him. I liked the look of the player and with my knowledge of what clubs and managers look at for players in his position I decided he was worth the risk. I brought him to England and got him placed with a small team that give players like him a chance. My reputation, of course, helped to seal that deal as I do not bring in rubbish. He had a great season in which he stood out a mile from the opening day to the last, and he was duly sold to a big team last year. When I was selling him I made a big deal of the fact that he had played in some huge matches and that he was used to the pressure and hostility that go with that, so when he travels to Liverpool away or Manchester United away, he will have the temperament to handle the occasion.

"As of right now, a lot of solicitors could not have done that for him. They just don't have the intimate knowledge of football, the players within it and their individual situations. Yes, they are professional people but they are legal people."

@Markarthurs: *"If an agent has fallen out with a club, does this bar his players from that club?"*
"Great question. In my case definitely not, but I do not fall out with clubs. It is the way in which you let down the club that's important. If three clubs want to buy a player, two of them will miss out. If the ultimate decision is based on sound reasons, then, as disappointed as the other two clubs will be, they should accept it because that's business. As for some other agents, though, human nature might impact on a thought process. The agent should be acting in the best interests of the player but all parties recognise their roles; everybody wants what

is best for each of them but occasionally one party will do better out of a deal than another.

"At one particular club, I took their leading light on a Bosman free to a bigger club. I got the player three or four times his salary and he was delighted. The manager understandably was not happy and his mood was not helped when, the following season, I took his side's next best player out of the club on exactly the same deal. He, too, was delighted. The parting conversation with that manager was explosive, to say the least, and while he didn't exactly say, 'The next time I see you I'll rip your fucking head off,' he might as well have.

"Twelve months later that same manager was at a different club and wanted a player that I represented. It's the only meeting I've ever been to where I didn't know how it was going to go. I told myself that if he growled at me, he would show himself up in front of the player that he was desperate to sign. At the meeting, he was as nice as pie to me; he shook my hand and couldn't have been more charming. But it wasn't that he didn't want to show himself up in front of the player – it was purely business. That's the game.

"When I was learning my way in the trade over 15 years ago, I did a deal in which I thought that the manager I was negotiating with had got the better of me. I took that personally and told him so. After the meeting we stepped outside the room and he completely changed persona – he grabbed my arm and said, 'Listen, step back and look at it. It's just business – don't take it personally.' That was a very valuable lesson at the time. Agents and managers and even clubs can fall out in the moment but there is too much business to be done for any animosity to linger."

@Rideitnow: *"Do you have to be a greedy bastard, or does it just help if you are?"*

"There are two answers to this question. The first answer is: fuck off, stop being jealous and take a bit of time to educate yourself about an industry that I'm quite sure you know nothing about. The second answer would be: it helps if you are a good negotiator and under-stand the requirements of clubs, players and the industry. It's no good having three parties sat around the table who are all happy with the deal if the fourth party isn't, because that kills it. You have to negoti-ate. There are some greedy bastards and sharks out there who will screw the player over, but that is true of any business. A good agent negotiates and leaves the table with every party happy with the deal.

"In my view, this question could have been worded a hundred different ways but the fact that it was worded in this way is indicative of a public who are ill-informed and spoon-fed by a media that are on the outside looking in, as much as they like to think otherwise.

"There is a lot of skill in what I do. It's not an art but it is demand-ing – you need to be switched on all the time. Negotiating is a very high-level craft: say the wrong thing at the wrong time and you can kill a deal. But if you say the right thing and recognise when people in the room have sat up and taken notice and you know how to follow up, then you will win more than you lose. It's like poker but with a lot more skill to it.

"There are one or two merciless people, just as there are in every industry. In our industry, however, we are still stuck with this notion that this is the people's game, and those people are working-class and that means that nobody is allowed to make 'obscene amounts of money'. But the money is already there; if it wasn't, we wouldn't get paid what we do.

"We are still fans; we all cheered England on at Euro 2012. We just have to look at football in a slightly different way. In fairness, it isn't only fans who have a preconception where agents are concerned. I've been to meetings where the manager has introduced me to the coach and he has refused to shake my hand because I am an agent. He probably doesn't use one because he doesn't trust them, but I assure you that if he had employed me, he would have a better contract than the one he has now.

"All that aside, if you do have the balls to run your own business and the inclination to get off your arse and chuck yourself in at the deep end, then go out and get your agent's licence and have a go at it. Anybody is allowed to be an agent; on reflection, maybe that's a problem."

@T_nic: "How are the interests of multiple clients handled evenly? Especially if they're after the same position at the same club."
"All agents are different, obviously, but from my point of view I treat all my players equally – as if they are the most important client I have. When a player wants a move, I will put his name forward to every club that I think is suitable for him. If he asks me to approach a specific club that I know isn't right for him, I will do as he asks but I will also explain the reasons it may not be a good move. The buying club will decide which player they want anyway, but the ultimate decision always rests with the player.

"My players tend not to overlap each other, so even if I have two left backs they will each have their own distinctive set of attributes.

Clubs are very specific in what they want from a player and so my two left backs could be separated by age, the size of the transfer fee, the size of their wages and so on. And within that there will be other considerations such as a team's style of play and whether the player will need to push on and have pace or stay back and defend.

"Let's take tall strikers as an example – or number 9s, as we used to call them. All of them will have different attributes despite playing the same position, and they are surprisingly easy to separate once a club looks at the nitty-gritty. Sometimes a team's tactics will dictate: if you're just going to bang the ball in the box, then you don't want the player with the better feet; you want the player who primarily heads the ball on. Another striker might play better on his own and yet another may run the channels more than any of the others.

"If I have Patrice Evra and Ashley Cole as clients and each of their wages are similar, their ages are similar and tactically they are the same, then I will still put them both in to the buying club and leave the club to make their decision. Look at it another way: if a club want a left back and I only have Patrice Evra, that means that another agent will have Ashley Cole and he is going to put his client forward for consideration, so we're still going to be fighting the same battle.

"But I know the mentality of the managers. I know if my players prefer a hug or if they work better after they get an almighty bollock-ing. Some players are motivated by an 'in-your-face' manager, whereas some are very bright and tactically aware and they like to engage at a high level with the manager because they have contributions and ideas of their own to make. This is a very stereotypical example, obviously, and it isn't quite as clear-cut as this, but each player lends himself to the right manager. Some of my players come to me when it is time to move and ask only to go to a club where the manager doesn't get in your face very much, and vice versa."

@Smithy_NUFC: "Do agents think there should be more transparency with financial details, or should they remain private?"
"I know this refers to agents' deals but the issue of transparency extends right across football. This may surprise one or two people but the clubs themselves are not overly keen on having too much transparency where their dealings are concerned, especially when it comes to transfers.

"The reason some transfers are reported as undisclosed is surprisingly simple. Sometimes the buying club will feel they have overpaid for a player (maybe they were held to ransom on deadline day or the manager was extremely insistent). The knock-on effect is that the club may not get their money back when it comes to sell that player again; it could even be the case that they pay £10m and get back £2m after the player's move doesn't work out. It stands to reason, then, that the people who did the deal in the first place don't want to be seen as having got it wrong. Very often a selling club will say that the deal was £10m by building in all the add-ons that they stand to make if the player is successful at his new club, and their fans think, 'Great, that's a good price for him.' The buying club, however, will say that the price paid was £6m by only admitting to the upfront payment and their fans think, 'Great, that's a good price for him.'

"The industry is such that some deals just don't work out. There are a variety of reasons, such as a change of manager or tactics, players not settling in to an area or simply a loss of form. Each club simply has to get more decisions right than wrong.

"Sometimes it will work the other way when a selling club in the lower leagues desperately need the money and sell off their prized asset on the cheap. Understandably, they wouldn't want their fans or the media to see that the owners are not getting value for money for their assets. Undisclosed deals help to protect the guys at the club doing the deals: they protect their jobs and they protect their reputation.

"As far as agents are concerned, my job is not in the public sector. It is private and I don't care what anybody else earns, so I don't see why my wages should be for public consumption, much in the same way that the wages of an accountant are not. How much do you earn? What are your bonuses? It isn't anyone's business but your own, right? Clubs don't want you to know about their business transactions. Remember, most of them are not listed on the stock exchange; they are private companies. The players don't want you to know what they earn, so why would agents?

"A very well-known pundit wrote in his newspaper column that players should not have agents, because if all wages were disclosed there would be no need for them. This ex-player was privileged to play at one club for his entire career and used an accountant to look after his affairs. Two things follow from that: firstly, would the accountant have been able to generate a move for the player if he needed it? It's not just a matter of phoning a club and offering a player. If you are not known in the industry, you won't receive a return call. Secondly, can you imagine what would happen if all wages were disclosed? Imagine sitting next to a player in the changing room who you don't rate and is half the player you are, knowing that he's on double the wage that you are. It's a known fact that players discuss wages, despite the fact that club rules prevent such disclosure, but how many players tell their team-mates the truth about what they earn? If wages were disclosed, can you imagine the disharmony in the dressing room?"

@Case_paul: *"How do you see the role of agents changing in the next 10 years?"*

"I really don't see it changing at all, but from an administrative point of view the FA, Fifa and Uefa have a view on that. Fifa wanted to deregulate the agency world and introduce intermediaries who are not licensed, which in theory means that anybody can represent a player. The onus would be on the player and the club to make sure that that intermediary is trustworthy. The thought process behind that is to deregulate an industry that is difficult to monitor. For example, in South America third-party ownership is common practice but in Europe it is illegal. Uefa don't want third-party ownership because it is a minefield, as shown by the Carlos Tévez saga a few seasons ago. That was one example that ended up with the need for new laws and resulted in lawsuits between clubs.

"Fifa believe that a significant number of deals involve unlicensed agents. The unlicensed agent is a problem and while rule changes in the last couple of years have helped the situation in the UK, it still remains a problem. If an agent is unlicensed then it allows the operator to act outside the rules; the only problem he then has is getting the deal signed off by a licensed agent. This was not uncommon in the past but new rules have been introduced to make this far more difficult, with penalties and fines for clubs and agents that sign off on deals with unlicensed agents. The FA do a good job in this country and our market is probably better regulated than any other, but we still need significant improvement as there are many ways to abuse the rules. The exams in this country are difficult and well controlled, so perhaps that could be the reason that some UK-based operators go to the well-known football hotbeds of Sierra Leone or Barbados to obtain a licence and then register as an overseas agent, which enables them to operate here.

"There is an army of unlicensed agents out there and the reason many remain so is that it is much easier to avoid regulation. Also, if you fail the exam twice you can't take it again for another two years. The exam is every six months, so in theory if you failed twice but wanted to set up an agency legitimately you could well be waiting three years before you can start. Meanwhile you've lost all your players to other agencies."

@Stuartgreen747: "How is it possible to represent both parties in a transfer? Surely there is a conflict of interest?"

"The rules have changed a couple of times in the last decade. The Inland Revenue questioned whether it was a ploy to save players tax when agents were continually acting for the club; in reality though, they were acting for the player. The current rules allow dual representation that accurately reflects what happens in a deal. Let's say a club wants a player that I represent, in order for dual representation to take place. The player, if he hasn't already done so in writing with the agent, must provide written consent allowing the agent to provide his services to the club. Once the agent has that player's consent, the player, club and agent all sign and register a form called an AGPC with the FA. Once the FA acknowledges the form, the agent is then able to enter into a contract with the club and provide it with services. A deal is only concluded if all parties agree and so the agent, by providing services to the club, while representing the best interests of his player, negotiates a deal that is acceptable to all. The Inland Revenue has recognised that the agent is providing a genuine service to both parties, while the club pays the agent. The player is only taxed on the element of the services provided to the player.

"I'm talking as a genuine, honest agent here: there isn't a conflict of interest if the agent has the best interests of the player at heart and acts in a professional manner."

@Bluemorbo: "What are the most difficult demands you've ever had to deal with from a player or club?"

"When I was starting out and learning the ropes, a senior player once asked me for front-row seats to a Madonna concert that had been sold out for two months. It had to include the after party and backstage passes, of course. I got those tickets through the biggest tout in the country and they cost me a fortune; on top of that you wouldn't believe the time and effort that it took to secure them – it was ridiculous. In the end, the player had to attend a rearranged match and so he didn't even go to the show. He just gave the tickets away to some friends and didn't even offer them back to me. It was a big lesson in life. I have never done anything like that again, and I never will."

@ *TheTallyVic*: *"How much are agents involved in investing players' money?"*

"If you're an IFA (independent financial advisor), then you'll be involved heavily, mainly by filtering money into tax-saving schemes. This first came about when agents who were looking to do well for their top clients but didn't know anything about investments brought their players to IFAs in return for a fee. Naturally, greed got the better of the IFAs and before long they had removed the agent from the equation altogether and were not only handling the players' investments but also trying to do their contracts. As I mentioned, though, in the early days these IFAs had no clue how football deals were done, and many of them still don't. Their clients lost fortunes through poor deals, and most of them are now facing huge tax bills as the revenue catches up with the tax-saving schemes that were recommended by the IFAs.

"I have never told my players that they must invest in something, because I am not an investment expert and would not be comfortable if those investments did not work out. My players will sometimes bounce investments that they are looking at off me and I will either say, 'It looks good but it's your call,' or, 'Don't touch it because...' but always the player will have to follow his own advice.

"Players will very often look for their own investments such as property and wine, both of which are fairly low-risk given the sums involved and the earning power of the players. But I have seen players who have lost everything and I have seen players go against my advice to not do something and end up doing very well. Imagine having somebody's bankruptcy on your conscience."

The Secret Footballer: "What is meant by hijacking deals, and does this happen?"

"It does happen – far more often than people would imagine. It is where another agent tries to get involved in a deal. This may be ringing clubs claiming to represent players that they don't, in the hope that they will find a club for that player. If they do get interest, or even if they don't, a call is made to the player in the hope that they can get involved in a deal. This is a tactic often used by new entrants to the agency world, those without many clients and those who have questionable morals. If the player's agent is acting as he should, then he will be making those calls already and the hijacker is adding no value and is, in fact, in breach of FA rules and regulations. I have a very good working relationship with all my clients, so this is not a problem for me. Normally my players, or even clubs, will tell me if some other agent has been on the phone to them trying to get involved.

"This business is based on relationships. Where a particular agent has a close relationship with a club that he has done a lot of business with, he can act for the club on a retainer or he can act for the manager. When attempting to negotiate a deal for a player that one agent might represent, it is not uncommon for another agent to act for the buying club. That's not hijacking – that's a legitmate part of the business. Hijacking is when the other agent claims to be representing a player that he isn't, or he tries to get involved and 'attends the party without an invite'."

The Secret Footballer: "What happens when agents and players fall out?"
"Players are contracted to an agent for anything up to two years. Most agency contracts do not allow the player to terminate the contract early, which in part protects the agent – but rightly so if he has nurtured a talent and looked after his interests. Players can easily be persuaded to sign with another agent and, while illegal, 'incentives' are used by many less scrupulous agents to obtain a signature.

"I have always believed that if you look after your clients, are open, honest and good at your job, the client will stay with you. Virtually all of my clients have stayed with me for this reason but there is always the odd exception. Some players are swayed and there are lots of different personalities and egos, hence some fall-outs are inevitable. Very often a club or another agent will encourage a player to attend a negotiation without his agent. The other agent doesn't care that the player has a contract with his existing agent as he will be acting for, and is paid by, the buying club. What happens between the player and his existing agent, though, is a fall-out.

Disputes are dealt with at the FA by what are known as Rule K tribunals. You would be amazed how many disputes arise in the football industry. There are a significant number of law firms occupied in such matters. FA rules and regulations are considered in these disputes, as are the contracts in place between each party, before, eventually, the tribunal reaches its decision. Most of these cases are not reported as they are conducted in private and not in the courts."

CHAPTER 8
MONEY

Talking about what you earn might be considered a little vulgar, especially if nine times out of ten the people you are speaking to can only dream of making what you do. Yet when I was kicking a flat ball around a council estate with holes in my Nike hand-me-downs, I was curious about players' wages, and as the seasons slip by, it seems fans are increasingly interested in little else. So let's talk money.

Be honest. How many of you, when berating a player either in the pub or in the stands, bring up money? Most, I'll bet. "Overpaid!" "Not worth it!" Rarely will anyone say the owners were mad to give him the wage in the first place. Instead, most of the anger goes towards the player, for having the sheer nerve to accept it. And this is what I don't understand, because in any walk of life, how many people say: "You know what? I think you're paying me too much." And there aren't many of us who would turn down the opportunity to leave a place of work and do the same job for somebody else if it meant a higher salary and a better standard of living for our families. So I try not to feel guilty – although I sometimes do – and I try not to feel that I have been greedy in any way. That is not to say that I don't "get" the argument of "How much is enough?" when people question why a player earning tens of thousands of pounds a week needs to ask for £10k, £20k, £30k more. But, as far as I'm aware, it is still illegal in this country for a player to hold a gun to a chairman's head. Shame, really.

The point I am trying to make is that football club owners, as much as players, drive wages. After all, a player can ask for as many zeros on the end of his salary as he wants but the only way he will get that money is if an owner is willing to pay it. To let you into my mind, when I find myself the subject of a transfer and subsequent contract negotiations, I try to remove all of the emotion and work on this simple principle: a group of business people have taken the decision that their club can afford to make me an offer of X amount of money over Y amount of years. If their business falls into decline, it is because those same people got their figures wrong or misjudged the market. Players can, of course, fail to live up to expectations, but can one bad signing bring down a football club?

Before I stand accused of portraying all footballers as the good guys, let me share a few things. Between you, me and the rest of the world, there are some players out there moving clubs every year to earn contract payoffs and signing-on fees. Some players see football purely in financial terms, exactly as people do in other professions. They play the game simply because it's a well-paid job. I have lost count of the number of times I have heard: "If I could get the same money doing something else, I'd be gone in a flash."

Every job has its perks, so why not try to enjoy the ones that come with playing football for millions of pounds? As the song goes, I like new cars, caviar and four-star daydreams but as for buying a football team, I'll leave that to the billionaires who spend eight-figure sums on players. And who cares where their money comes from? Not players and not many supporters – at least not until it goes wrong.

So what do fans really want? Players to give 100%? That's the easy answer. How about every trophy, every great player and the best coach possible? And it isn't enough to just win: if the football gods could throw in relegation or financial strife for your biggest rival, well, that would be even better.

So who is greedy, me? Possibly. The owners? In some cases, definitely. You? Well, I wouldn't say greedy, just superambitious, and there is certainly nothing wrong with that in life. But the next time you go to punch your pin in to buy three tickets to watch your team play, ask yourself what really makes you happy. Because those of you who want the very best talent that enables your team to compete and win trophies will know that somebody has to pay for it, and those same people will also understand that if it all ends in tears, it isn't necessarily the players who need shooting. For the most part, we're just playing our part in somebody else's grand design. Those who don't understand that argument: take your card out of the machine and take the kids to the park. Either way, the real power still belongs to you.

Our wages may be well out of sync with the man in the street's but why shouldn't they be? Hundreds of thousands of people are more than happy to pay to watch us each week, the kids in the park want to emulate us by wearing shirts with our names emblazoned across the back, and the sponsors and sports manufacturers are desperate to get into bed with us because it sells product (mums and dads often ask me who my boots are made by because their child has asked for a pair just like mine for Christmas or a birthday).

I can't understand the people who trot out that tired cliché that money has ruined football. How? Nobody has spent more money than Manchester City and yet the way in which the team sealed their first title for 44 years, with a minute left on the clock and their fiercest rivals thinking that they had done enough, gave us arguably the greatest climax to the most enthralling Premier League season since its inception in 1992. In fact, in terms of league victories in this country it may even surpass the Arsenal triumph at Anfield in 1989.

And I want to see Manchester City compete with Manchester United. I want to see derby matches that mean something more than just local pride. I want to see the best players plying their trade in this country. I was gutted to see Ronaldo go to Real Madrid (although, having played against him, I can say that he is a diver, as I have told him several times), because it would be nice to think that we can attract the best players to these shores and keep them here when they're in their prime.

I have to agree with my peers that most of the resentment towards players from the fans is jealousy, which is brought about by two things. Firstly, a football club is nothing without its fan base – in general terms, the bigger the fan base, the larger the club. Owners come and go but countless families are tied to their club by history and geography. The fans may not own the club but, in a very real way, it belongs to them, it belongs to the community. All of which means that if a player doesn't play well, the fans will feel it personally. And I can guarantee that the first thing that everybody will hold against that player will be the size of his transfer fee and his wages.

A good friend of mine who is the chairman of a big northern club once said to me, after I'd offended him by introducing him as the owner of the club: "I am not the owner; I am the custodian." Later he explained: "The football club belongs to the people of the town. I am simply looking after it in the best way that I can and I hope to hand it over to the next custodian in much better shape than when it was handed over to me." So I do understand that argument.

The second thing is that we are still seen as an intellectually inferior group of people, and in this country intellectually inferior people are viewed with contempt if they happen to do well for themselves. We didn't work hard at school, we aren't great conversationalists, we don't curve our vowels and we certainly aren't going to find a cure for cancer. Apparently, our talent doesn't really count because of the perception that we were born with it, which is bullshit. There seems to be the feeling that those who went to private school and were born of blue blood can be tolerated in positions of highly paid work because that's the way it's always been. Because of the people who populate the jobs and the people who watch the game, football is still considered, rightly or wrongly, to be a working-class sport. And some of the fans seem to be having a tough time adjusting to the fact that members of their own class are escaping the status quo. For a nation that prefers to pull people down rather than propel them on, that is a bitter pill to swallow and gives rise to desperate feelings of isolation and worthlessness. I could be talking rubbish but that's what it feels like.

It is a brave new world, and for me there is no such thing as being paid too much. There are only jobs that pay a salary. If you fall below the standard, you will soon be found out.

So how do some of these huge wages and transfer fees come about? When a manager sits down with his scouts and coaching staff he will work from what is known, unspectacularly, as "the list". Every player will be on a list at one club or another – it is simply a question of the position.

Let's say that a manager is looking for a striker in the summer transfer window. Depending upon how hands-on he is (some like to do everything themselves, including dealing with agents for reasons that I'm sure you can guess), he will give his director of football or chief executive the name of the number one target on his list. It is then the responsibility of this person to speak to the agents and the player to see if he has an interest in joining before an official approach is made to his club. (This is completely illegal but it is the way it's done at almost every club.) If word comes back that the player is too expensive or simply does not want to leave his present club, then the manager and his colleagues will work their way down the list until they find an available player within their budget. It is not uncommon to end up at number four or five on the list.

This is how it happens at every club. It's archaic, I know, but somehow it works. This also goes some way to explaining why some deals come out of thin air and at the last minute. Very often you might see a club linked with the same footballer all through the summer but at the 11th hour they sign someone completely different. Often what has happened is that the number one target has played the field before deciding to sign for a different club. Still in desperate need of a new striker, the manager works his way down the list until he finds a player who is available and fits the criteria. Think how many press conferences you have seen where the player says, "I was just about to go on holiday and suddenly out of the blue my agent rings me..." Now you know why – he was your club's 10th-choice striker.

As a young player desperate for some attention, I used to be excited about being on another club's list but only because it felt like an acknowledgement that I was doing something right. Of course, the older you get and the more well known you become, the more lists you are going to be on.

This is how it generally works. Ten Premier League clubs might be looking for a striker in the summer, so they each draw up a list. Half of those 10 clubs might be on the lookout for a tall striker and half again might want a proven centre forward rather than one who will need a few years to polish up and, possibly, sell on for a large transfer fee. Those clubs might be prepared to offer huge wages, rather than a huge transfer fee, pushing them towards Bosmans.

If you're really lucky you might be on that list. If you're incredibly lucky and all the stars are lined up just right, then you may even be the number one target. But nothing in football is ever straightforward. I've finished seasons having performed really well but not been able to reap the rewards of a move because I've had a couple of years left on my contract and my club had no interest in selling. If I'd been on a free, I could probably have doubled my wages. A former team-mate of mine was much more fortunate and set himself up for life after finding himself in the right place at the right time.

There are other factors that can help. For example, many clubs will try to only use a particular agent and, therefore, do a disproportionate number of deals with players whom that agent represents or can get access to. In the case of the latter, if the agent does not represent the player, then he will approach the agent who does and try to work a deal by offering him the move in return for a cut. The bottom line is that, if a club offer you a king's ransom every week, you had better make sure you take it because if you don't, there are 100 other players who will.

We all want to extract the most from our bosses and we all want the best for ourselves, no matter what job we do and where we live. I don't want my kids to grow up on a council estate like I did – not because there is any shame in that, but simply because I don't want their success to be measured by being able to just about afford the mortgage and holding a job down at the local factory and having a week's holiday in Spain every three years. Some people are happy with that and that's perfectly fine, but I'm not and I wouldn't be for my children either.

So if my employer offers me a pay rise, I'm going to take it. The bigger picture is not how well I can live and how many pointless possessions I can accumulate but what sort of start in life I can give my children and their children. So if I earn £100,000 a week and my club offers me £110,000, I'm going to take it and I know you would too.

Players don't have any moral obligation to a club's finances. If a club falls on hard times or, worse, goes bust, it is unfortunate but it isn't our fault. Fortunately, in the Premier League at least, there is plenty of money around. To prove the point, look at the transfer fees being paid for players who could be considered a punt. Not too long ago the fee for that player would have been about £1m–2m but today it is more like £5m–10m. In fact, the clubs right at the top can afford to write off huge losses if players don't perform: Robbie Keane (£18m to Liverpool), Andriy Shevchenko (£30m to Chelsea), Emmanuel Adebayor and Roque Santa Cruz (£24m and £19m respectively to Manchester City) all struggled after these moves. But what difference has it made really? Manchester City tried a host of strikers before getting it right with Agüero. Remember Jô and Caicedo, £17m and £7m respectively? I couldn't even tell you where they are now.

But the numbers at City are unrivalled anywhere in the world. I was talking to one of the senior figures a few years ago and mentioned that I was available for a very reasonable outlay. He laughed – out of pity, I think. After a couple of glasses of champagne, I asked what I thought was a cheeky question: "You're not really going to buy Kaká for £100m and give him £500k a week, are you? You'll bankrupt the club." He met it with a completely straight bat. "Let me put it to you in this way, my friend. Our fund is making about $100m a day from oil alone."

These people are in the top 0.1% of the richest in the world and so huge wages and vast transfer fees are not a problem. The net worth of the fund under the control of City's owners is said to be in the region of £550bn, and with these figures in mind it is no surprise that the wages in the Premier League are catching up with the NBA and the MLB, especially when you consider that the Premier League has a far larger global television audience. Is it any wonder that the league is attracting multinational investors? The sports-mad Americans clocked the potential before anybody else, naturally. The Glazers moved in to United, Liverpool have already had two sets of American owners, Aston Villa were purchased by the American billionaire Randy Lerner and Arsenal's majority shareholder, Stan Kroenke, is also American.

The byproduct of all that is that one should never feel guilty about asking for exorbitant wages because you never know who is holding the purse strings. There is a famous story about Seth Johnson's contract negotiations when he was about to sign for Leeds United. This was during the time when Leeds were living beyond their means in pursuit of success. Almost every single player in football, past and present, has a variation of this tale but the central features are not up for debate. The way I heard it was that Johnson had gone into negotiations with his agent looking for a three-year deal on £15,000 a week. Sat across the table were the representatives of Leeds United, including Peter Ridsdale, the chairman at the time, and none of them were in the mood to negotiate. "We'd like to offer you a five-year contract," they began, "at £37,000 a week and that's it." Johnson's agent asked for a moment with his client and promptly informed the player to sign the deal as quickly as possible.

So I ask the question: is that greed? What would you do? Come clean? I wouldn't. I would have done exactly the same as Johnson did – get my arse back in the room and sign the deal before anybody asked any awkward questions. When things went pear-shaped at Leeds there were a number of players who, despite having moved on, were still having their wages subsidised by their former club. An interview with Ken Bates, after he assumed control of Leeds and went over the books, revealed that every penny the club earned from its foray to the semi-final of the Champions League (about £12m) went in wages to Gary Kelly over his five-year contract. And this, remember, is a right back. I feel sorry for the Leeds fans but had I been one of their players at the time, I would have had no sympathy for the people who handed out the telephone-number contracts. The problem for the players is that we are the public face of failure – there is nowhere to hide on a football pitch. But as an owner there is the tinted glass at the top of the stadium or, much more in vogue today, a different country entirely. Take a bow, the Glazers.

Years ago, when there were far more bidding wars for run-of-the-mill players, many that I knew were benefiting from "parity" contracts. These were put in place to entice players to sign for one team over another with the guarantee that no matter who the club then signed – Shearer, Giggs, Keane etc – the player would always be paid the same as the highest earner. Those who had them really did laugh all the way to Coutts.

These contracts first appeared in the late 90s, which was the first problem. At this point Premier League clubs had still to attract the super-rich owners that we see today, but when they did take over, wages went through the roof and any player with a parity contract reaped the rewards. Today such contracts are few and far between but there are still one or two to be found. Carlos Tévez is said to have a clause in his contract that ensures he remains City's highest-paid player. If City were in the market for someone like Messi, in the same way that they were with Kaká a few years ago, Tévez would more than likely double his wages. While City would be able to afford it, giving a huge pay rise to a player who went awol during their pursuit of their first Premier League title would not go down well in Abu Dhabi. This highlights one of the dangers with parity contracts. And try to imagine if you had been at City all season and played an influential part in the club's first championship for 44 years (I'm thinking Joe Hart,

David Silva, Agüero, Vincent Kompany) only to see Tevez double his money after the club signed Messi in the summer. In other words, parity contracts breed resentment among other players and can be more trouble than they're worth. Unless you've got one, of course.

Footballers' new-found wealth has opened up a host of recreational possibilities, and not just for the highest-earners. Horse racing has always been a staple pastime of the footballer but now it's done in serious style, with players helicoptered in from all corners of the country and waited on hand and foot in the most sought-after boxes with the best food and drink available.

A few years ago around 20 of us piled down to the Cheltenham Festival. I had never been before and didn't know what to expect. I didn't think I'd enjoy it but I had always wanted to go, just so I could say I had. As it turned out, it was a great day and something that I'd like to do again, albeit perhaps not in quite the same style. The day started at 6.30am outside the training ground, where a white limousine (classy) picked us up before driving for what felt like hours to the festival. Anyone who was late had to have a Jägerbomb, anyone who phoned their wife or girlfriend had to have a Jägerbomb, and every hour on the hour, everyone had to have a Jägerbomb. The upshot was that by the time we arrived in Cheltenham (missing the first race), we were well on the way to infamy. Stepping out of the limo and into a load of tweed was about as uncomfortable as it is possible for me to feel. I'd much rather blend in but when 20 footballers are marching towards the main stand you do tend to stick out a little.

In every squad there are one or two who really know their stuff or, at the very least, know someone who knows their stuff. In our group we had such a man. I don't know where he was getting the calls from but as soon as he won the second race, I held on to his coat-tails and didn't let go. Everyone quickly jumped on the bandwagon, until eventually this player had to offer his disclaimer: "If you're gonna follow me, don't blame me if you lose. I'm not saying that you should bet on these horses, OK? And I'm not really comfortable." To which the captain replied: "Just shut up and give us the tips." Each player took it in turns to place the bet and by the fifth race there was a large sum of money building up in the middle of the table.

Behind us was a table of tweed that, in fairness, we were probably annoying with our raucous behaviour. But it's a day at the races on the Guinness (and the Jägerbombs), so people are going to let their hair down, aren't they? Each time the noise levels grew, this table would turn around in unison and breathe a collective sigh of disgust. It wasn't long before our table began to take offence at their taking offence and out of that was born one of the finest examples of putting people in their place that I have ever witnessed.

By this point our confidence was running away with us and we collectively staked £10,000 on an each-way that duly came in. The money was dumped in the middle of the table and by now had grown to at least £50,000, probably more. As we were all sitting around congratulating ourselves, there was a big laugh from the table of tweed, one of those laughs that you know has just come at your expense. A couple of the lads turned around to be met by a well-to-do lady who said to them, "That will get you plenty of Wags." It didn't even make sense but it was delivered with such a nasty twang that the entire table took exception to it.

None more so, however, than our star player. He reached across into the middle of our table and picked up a wedge, turned around and ripped the notes in half before throwing them up in the air to rain down all over the woman and her guests. At the time, it was cringeworthy. But when I got home and sobered up, I concluded that it was almost the perfect response from those with the new money to those with the old – a feeling that was reinforced when I recalled the sight of the other table passing around a roll of tape to stick the notes back together. Sometimes, no matter what you do to try to change people's minds, they will have an unshakable prejudice against you. And although our star player lived up to the stereotype, his actions had shown these people up for what they were.

As you've seen, you can't talk about horse racing without mentioning gambling. Gambling and football are inseparable. I'm not a massive gambler but even I used to do pretty well coming up with Champions League accumulators before the governing bodies changed the law to prevent players betting on any sport that they were involved in. I didn't study the form guides or anything like that – I just went with my gut reaction – and I only gambled about £100 a time.

A few seasons ago, I roomed with the real thing on a tour of the Middle East. We were together for a week, and I promise you the only thing that either of us said to the other in that time was, "Have you got the key for the room?" I had heard this player had a bit of an issue with gambling but I had never seen anything like this. He had brought two laptops with him and plugged them both in on the desk. My hopes of Skyping home didn't get a look-in. I'm still unsure why he had two laptops rather than just having a couple of tabs open. There was

Betfair and Paddy Power and on top of that he had his mobile phone set to receive live sports updates, and he was betting on anything and everything. Thankfully he did eventually get the help that he needed.

The saddest gambling story I ever heard involved two Newcastle players who would kill time in hotel rooms before games by betting big money on which raindrop would fall from the top of the window frame first.

The advent of online gambling has brought with it new temptations for players looking to cash in and, just like the parity contracts, it's about being in the right place at the right time. When I started playing professionally, in-play betting had just come to the market; nobody really knew if it was going to take off but that didn't stop every bookmaker from offering its own version. The service has been refined in the intervening years to maximise the bookies' profits but there was a small window of opportunity where the punters and the players were able to take advantage.

An old team-mate of mine was one beneficiary. Throughout the season a team will usually win the toss 50% of the time, but away from home, even if the captain loses the toss, the home team will forfeit the kick-off so that they can kick towards their own fans in the second half. If you intentionally go after the kick-off and you don't care which end you kick towards first, then you could easily end up with 75% of the kick-offs over the course of a season. And if that happens, then it becomes ridiculously easy to bet on which team will win the first throw-in.

As a young, naive kid, I simply thought that this player was hopeless. We'd take the kick-off and pass it back to him and every time, without exception, he'd hit the ball towards the touchline and out of play. It was so easy that nobody noticed and it wasn't until years later, when a few of us from that team were talking about the old days, that it dawned on me what had been going on. Whenever I tell that story to a player who was also plying his trade back then, his reply is usually always the same: "Oh yeah, we had a lad that used to do that, too. He made a fortune." I have heard of the same being done with corners, goal kicks, fouls and even yellow cards.

As online gambling took off, however, buoyed by the success of in-play betting, the algorithms that powered it became ever more sophisticated. Today, websites will detect new users, irregular sums (which could mean a group of players has staked different amounts, resulting in an odd total) or an unusual surge of betting from one country or even a row of houses in the same street. They will automatically track your betting history and some will even perform a credit check without you realising.

That doesn't mean players have stopped gambling altogether; it's just a question of finding a mule. I know of one team who regularly gambled on the outcome of their matches. They would only bet that they would win the match and there was no suggestion that they had engaged with any of the players from the opposition or had entered into any backhanded arrangements with them. But, money being money, it's easy to believe that the prospect of picking up some decent cash, outside of the win bonus, served as an incentive to put on better performances.

Don't for one minute think that this is an isolated incident. My guess is that this is happening up and down the country every single week and at some of our biggest clubs. I know players who are international team-mates and friends of players at other clubs, who are forever ringing each other while we're on the coach or at the hotel to ask: "How are you boys looking for tomorrow? Are you worth a punt?" These guys are studying the fixtures every weekend and picking out games that they fancy. If you have an inside track, it makes it slightly easier. Very often some of those players will ring to ask about our chances. Injury news is available to everyone through Sky Sports and various websites; what isn't is information such as which players were out on the piss on Thursday, which have been shacked up in a hotel room all week with a young lady, and which are experiencing problems at home.

Unsurprisingly, some of the biggest gamblers are at the biggest clubs. It is extremely difficult to keep tabs on – almost impossible in fact – but it is reassuring to see that, when it comes into the public domain, the authorities don't mess around. The investigation into match-fixing in Italy at the end of the 2011-12 season is a case in point.

The PFA has done a lot of great work to help players who have fallen into the pitfalls of gambling and addiction. They have helped many of my friends who have struggled in retirement, offering career advice and guidance on the options outside football. Some of my friends have invested rashly and had their fingers badly burned. Years ago, a lot of people were putting their cash into the British film industry and construction projects because of tax breaks. Some players made a lot of money but gradually Gordon Brown, who was chancellor at the time, began to close these tax loopholes. Some of my friends were left severely exposed and even lost their initial stake. One team-mate lost 300 grand and had to borrow from another player to bail himself out.

Regardless of how much money you've got to start with, investing is about having the conviction to back something that you believe in. There is a perception that footballers, because of their wealth and lack of experience, are vulnerable to financial sharks. In some cases that is true but the biggest danger they face when investing money is each other. The dressing room culture is that everyone wants to be in on everyone else's business, whether that's cars, girls or finance. If one player brings in an investment opportunity on the Monday, you can guarantee that, by the end of the week, everyone in the squad will know all about it and a fair percentage of them will be swayed by what others are doing, rather than their own due diligence. I remember how, when a famous stadium was redeveloped and turned into luxury apartments, the majority of our players snapped the properties up. I'd just signed at the time and – fortunately, as it turned out – wasn't in a position to buy one myself. But even then I remember thinking, why would I purchase a buy-to-let where I know I will immediately be up against 20 landlords each trying to find a tenant? You didn't have to be a financial wizard. The risks were obvious.

The players eventually got desperate and started to lower their demands to try to attract a tenant. And the same dressing room culture that led them to purchase a flat in the first place now led them to reveal what they were charging in rent. In the end they couldn't even cover the mortgages. When they all panicked and tried to flip the properties and recover their outlay, they encountered exactly the same problem and, ultimately, ended up in negative equity and writing off tens of thousands of pounds.

I know many footballers who made a fortune in property when the housing market was booming. By the same token, I know a lot of play-ers who suffered enormous losses when the bubble burst in 2008. But don't rush to feel sorry for them. The truth is that everybody has their hands out, especially in the Premier League, where everything is for the taking. I have come to realise there is just as much to be said for contentedness as there is for adding another zero on to the bank account. After all, how much is enough?

CHAPTER 9
BAD BEHAVIOUR

Let me say right at the top of this chapter that I am not whiter than white and have never pretended to be. In the days when I used to go out regularly, there were times when I was extremely irresponsible. I offended people with my behaviour and I have done some downright stupid things that I'm not proud of. But, on the other hand, it makes for a great collection of stories.

No matter who I have gone out with, I have always been known as the person in the group who can smell trouble. Wherever I am, I will be the one declining the lap dance, steering the others away from those who are looking to cause trouble and generally making sure we all finish the evening without too much distress caused to ourselves or others. I am extremely comfortable in my own company; I probably prefer it, if I'm honest, and I don't need a load of hangers-on massaging my ego. Like all recovering revellers, however, I am prone to the odd relapse. Everybody needs to let their hair down once in a while.

The money that players earn makes anything a possibility on a night out. One of the best ended with half a dozen of us waking up to an Amsterdam sunrise. On that occasion, we had ditched London because there was a rail strike and so the city was virtually deserted. After a quick "board meeting" we reconvened at Luton airport, and most of us were picking out a lady of the night before the early hours.

My parents instilled the belief in me that, if I were to do something stupid, like drugs, excessive alcohol or mass orgies that ended in unplanned pregnancies, I would always be the one that something terrible happened to, while everyone else would get away with it. (In truth, mass orgies and unwanted pregnancies is the only one that stuck with me, for some reason.) I have never even had a lap dance because I can't see the point of getting myself all worked up without the end product. I realised some time ago that it is just a question of price, but even so I have steered clear.

So I ended up in a café across the street while the others flew the flag for their respective countries. I was in there for about 20 minutes before I realised that I was breathing in a potentially lethal dose of Colombian woodbine that would be sure to interest the drug testers. Those are the little things that can trip you up: stupid things like that are forever happening to me, even when I'm trying to avoid trouble. And when I do let my guard down, things have a habit of going spectacularly wrong.

Over the past few years, Las Vegas has overtaken Marbella as the number one destination for footballers looking to let their hair down. There are plenty of reasons for this: the pool parties are insane, the girls are glamorous and there is nothing that a person can't have so long as he has the money to pay for it. But the real reason for fleeing to Vegas is obvious: out here, even our worst behaviour looks sedate.

Rehab is perhaps the best known of all the Vegas pool parties, and with a cabana costing around $10,000 per day, it is certainly the most expensive. On Sundays, the place is heaving with the beautiful people. A few seasons ago, I made the pilgrimage with a group of regular revellers and was blown away by the debauchery. By the end of the week, two players had gone home after simply not being able to take any more, eight players had new tattoos and one player took a local girl back to England and married her in a shotgun wedding. Halfway through the trip, one of the players said that Lindsay Lohan had invited us to her house in Los Angeles. After a quick meeting, they decided to hire a car and drive there – something that didn't appeal to me. That turned out to be a great decision because upon their arrival they quickly realised that she was under house arrest. As one of the lads later told me, "We drove five hours to watch a fucking movie." Idiots.

I've been to just about every club and trendy bar worth going to and I've seen every kind of show. I've done all the big nights in Ibiza at Pacha, Space, Amnesia and El Paradis. I've been all over Asia and partied in the trendiest parts of Tokyo and I've done everything worth doing in Britain and most of Europe, including ice bars in Sweden and burlesque shows in Paris. I went to a great bar in Estonia that doubled as a shooting gallery. After a few cocktails the waiters come round with a menu showing every type of gun imaginable; you simply choose a picture of a famous dictator, pick out a gun (I chose an AK-47) and away you go. I don't know what the fun police would make of it over here but it was a great experience. Taking all that in to account, I can honestly say that I have never seen a place quite like TAO in Las Vegas.

We took a table that had a $5,000 minimum spend, which isn't a problem as bottles of Dom Perignon are about $1,500. In Vegas, you absolutely must have a "sorter" – a type of concierge. This guy knows everyone in town, he will get you the best seats for shows, clubs, restaurants and pool parties, he'll have helicopters and limos on tap and access to all the women a man could ever need, as he proved on this night in TAO. As we took our seats, "Jess" introduced us to the owners and explained who we were. Five minutes later a parade of drop-dead-gorgeous women were walking in a line past our table. Each time we saw one that we liked we had to tell Jess, who would seat them at the table.

It was hugely embarrassing for me, but the girls make thousands of dollars a night and I'm not here to judge. Behind us was another table that included some proper stars, among them a Barcelona player. We had a couple more spaces to fill; when a woman who was a complete knockout walked past the table, everyone stood up in unison and yelled, "That one!" Shocking, isn't it?

Anyway, she had not gone unnoticed by the table behind and when Jess reappeared after being summoned by them, we realised that we were not quite as important as we thought we were. Jess told us: "The table behind have asked me to tell you that whatever you offer for this girl, they will double it." We pushed them to $5,000, which only served to embarrass everyone concerned because, as we later found out, it was not uncommon for some of these girls to attract around $30,000 in return for their company over the course of an evening. Anything outside of that was up to the discretion of the girl and subject to a fresh negotiation. At least that's what I heard.

But the close eye on the purse strings didn't last. In fact, from then on it went quite spectacularly in the opposite direction. One of our party, mortally offended at losing the girl to the table behind us, challenged them to a "champagne war". This is a legendary show of modern masculinity. If two tables begin to grate on one another, the idea is to send over a bottle of champagne; the other table is then meant to reciprocate, and on it goes until the bill gets too big for one side to pay. Effectively it's a game of poker with bluff and double bluff the key to winning. If a table keeps playing but cannot afford to pay they are forced into the ultimate loss of face – they are marched out of the club by security to heckles and wolf whistles.

My friend was not going to lose out twice in one evening. He summoned Jess and asked him to send the table a jeroboam of Cristal champagne, which he duly did. As the three-litre bottle made its way from the bar to the table, half the eyes in the place were following it on its journey. When our nemesis replied by sending a waitress over with exactly the same bottle plus 12 tequila shots, a cheer went up around the club and the champagne war was well and truly under way. Ten minutes later, my friend (nothing to do with me, and I made that clear to him at the time) sent back 10 regular-sized bottles of Cristal with a straw, an umbrella and a sparkler in each, only to be met almost instantly with an entire case (12 bottles) of 1998 vintage Dom Perignon. It's a slippery slope – the floor manager will automatically send more of the club's girls to sit down at each table to help drink it, thus keeping the war going, and each girl needs to be paid, of course.

Neither side showed any sign of giving up and, inevitably, my friend was able to rope in a few of the other players around our table to share the burden. Once that happened, bravado and bullshit came racing to the surface. "Let's just fucking blow them out the water," said one, and that's exactly what they did. On special occasions the club can "fly" bottles of champagne to any of the tables on wires. It looks spectacular and really ups the ante. The three of them told Jess to order the club's remaining five jeroboams of Cristal champagne and fly them over to the other table, and while they were in the air, the DJ had to press play on the iPhone that my friend had just given him. As I said earlier, so long as you can pay for it, Vegas will do anything for you.

As the first bottle made its way high above the crowd to a raucous reception and much American high-fiving by guys with caps on back to front, the DJ pressed play. I'm Forever Blowing Bubbles is a strange song for a football club to take as its anthem but stranger still is hearing it blaring from a Las Vegas nightclub in the early hours of the morning. The lads had tried to replicate the dambusters, which was why Jess had also been told to attach a union jack to each bottle as it flew over the dance floor. The show was not wasted on the table behind, who stood up and applauded. We sat and waited for the reply and a little later five empty bottles of Cristal went flying back over the dance floor with a white flag hanging out of each.

One of the members from the defeated table came down to shake our hands. I didn't recognise him but he was clearly a "somebody". He explained that he didn't want to leave the club but enough was enough. There was no way the owners would march him out because he was what Vegas calls a high roller, and a regular at this club. He offered to split the bill with us, which immediately got me thinking that we were yet another mark. In fact, I wouldn't have been surprised if he was the owner. The final bill? Just short of $130,000, excluding tip, which as Jess explained on the way back to the hotel was nowhere near the record but still a great effort.

Those situations can be awkward. I had made it clear that I did not want to participate but I was only kidding myself. How could I possibly sit at the table and buy my own drinks? It's ridiculous. I knew what the likely outcome of that night was going to be and I knew exactly what it meant to my finances to go to Las Vegas with another group of players. That's why I didn't put up any resistance as I checked out and paid the final bill of $14,000, which included some ridiculously overpriced room service and a helicopter trip to the Grand Canyon. The club is part of the hotel and, as such, any bill could simply be put on the room. Clearly somewhere along the way it had been split equally. Although I didn't moan, I did insist upon seeing everyone else's bill. That's just good business sense.

It wasn't the first time that I'd bumped into this Barcelona player. A few years earlier I was staying in his city on the weekend his team clinched the La Liga title. My wife and I had booked a room at the Gran Hotel La Florida with two of our dearest friends from England, a couple that we used to live near at the club I played for at that time. We spent the day relaxing by the pool, drinking mojitos and talking bullshit with the locals. That afternoon, my friend and I got talking to two very glamorous Catalan ladies who asked us what we did for a living, and we told them that we designed bars and restaurants (God knows why) and were in Barcelona to oversee our latest bar, called Luna-tic after the Spanish word for moon. The ladies were impressed and told us that they had their own company as interior designers and that they had worked on all the top bars in Barcelona, including the one we were now sitting in (what are the chances?). We even got an email from them when we returned home to say that they were very keen to talk to us about Luna-tic, and asking if we would be putting the interior design out to tender because they would very much like to quote for it.

Anyway, after a few more mojitos the hotel manager came into the bar to inform the guests that the entire place had been booked in advance. He apologised and suggested that perhaps we'd like to take a drink to the front of the hotel where, outside, they were hosting a vintage Ferrari convention. I admire Ferraris as much as the next man but when the hotel's resident tennis coach told me that the bar had been booked by Barcelona FC, I knew that there was only one place I was going to spend that evening. By hook or by crook, we were going to be in that bar. In the event it was incredibly easy to gatecrash: a team coach turned up and we simply followed the players into the bar. Far from being any kind of official function, it looked suspiciously like a spur-of-the-moment decision in the wake of the team's La Liga success. Suffice to say that, after some heavy drinking and watching the players jump in the pool with the trophy and some scantily clad ladies, we were accepted.

We partied on with the team and the majority of the other hotel guests for most of the night, pausing every now and again for a breather in the hotel lobby. During one break, a couple of the other players were chatting over a cigarette. My friend said that he had now had enough to drink to be past caring about being too polite to ask for pictures and, furthermore, he was going to his room to get his "good camera". But at the reception there were no staff, everybody was inside enjoying the party, the keys were locked away in little vaults behind the desk and there was no way of getting to them. The only thing in the lobby was an empty luggage trolley and before long we had challenged the two Barca players to a skate-off. Unfortunately, they agreed, probably drunk on the success of that La Liga title.

The game started off innocuously enough: skate to the other end of the lobby without falling off. But it wasn't long before the stakes were raised, with one of the club's Spanish midfielders suggesting, in remarkably good English, that a more difficult challenge would be to skate towards the revolving doors and time it so as to go straight through them and out into the car park. We agreed and the game started. At first it proved to be far too difficult but as each pairing had a few more goes, we all began to get closer until, eventually, the second Barca player sailed clean through and into the car park. We rushed through the doors after him just in time to see the trolley hit the cobbles and veer violently to the right, unseating its passenger before the front end of a Ferrari Testarossa stopped it dead. Thankfully, there was no damage to the luggage trolley – but the Ferarri was in a terrible state. The two poles at the front of the trolley had hit the car head on, and to anyone who hadn't witnessed the collision it would have appeared as if the owner had driven into a pair of parking bollards.

The next day we awoke – with a slight headache, I might add – and went downstairs to check out. At the desk there was an almighty row going on between the hotel staff and two very irate women, while a fair-sized crowd had also gathered. We were the only people checking out and the staff took us to the front so that we could get to the airport on time. As we got to the desk my friend nudged me and pointed to the two women causing the commotion. It was the interior designers that we'd floated the idea of Luna-tic past the previous afternoon. "What's the problem?" asked my friend. The women drew a heavy sigh, as if this was all they'd been talking about that morning, and between them told us what was going on. "We go into the town in the night-time yesterday for the opening of our new bar," said the first woman. "We place in there all the interior design," said the second. "When our driver brings us back in the hotel we notice our car is have a smash." And then, turning to the staff behind the desk, she continued: "And this bastards say we make the smash ourselves."

The man responsible is far more famous than me, far wealthier than me, and, to the best of my knowledge, has at least one more international triumph under his belt than me. But I'm not a total arsehole. I have promised myself that if I ever do decide to open Luna-tic in Barcelona, I will make sure those ladies get the contract for the interior design.

Air stewardesses have been a regular feature of more exotic nights out down the years, in particular since a player I knew started dating an Italian girl called Francesca who worked for Alitalia. She was – probably still is – absolutely stunning, a complete natural with a lot of class who gave me a penchant for air stewardesses from the moment I met her.

We have since crossed paths several times but by far and away the most memorable occasion was when her flight was grounded in London over Christmas while my team were staying in the capital ahead of a match. We smuggled the flight crew into our hotel and spent the rest of the evening getting to know one another. It wasn't long before the crew, tired and fed up, suggested a swim in the hotel's beautiful pool. None of the flight crew had their suitcases and so we had to seek out the kit man, who provided warm-up T-shirts and enough pairs of matchday shorts for all. (Kit men are great: they moan like drains if you actually ask for your kit but they always have your back. The next day this one had to explain to the manager why the shorts weren't entirely dry as we kicked off.)

Fully changed, the flight crew and several of the first-team squad went down to the pool. Francesca suggested playing Marco Polo, the game where one person closes their eyes while the others move around trying to avoid being grabbed. The person with their eyes shut calls out "Marco" and the others reply "Polo". Sounds shit, doesn't it? That's because it is. If a person leaves the pool, they automatically become a "fish out of water" and have to take their turn trying to catch the others. After half an hour or so, each end of the pool, the shower rooms, the sauna room and the jacuzzi were full of fish out of water. When Francesca turned to me to ask if I wanted to play just with her, I summoned some kind of superhuman strength and bid her a happy Christmas and a pleasant evening before heading back to my room to furiously take care of myself.

Christmas has always been an odd time of year but, personally, I love Christmas Day. I meet up with friends from all over the world before getting wrapped up nice and cosy to go outside to throw snowballs at each other. Then we'll come back in to warm up with a big mug of hot chocolate before having a turkey dinner with all the trimmings. But then training finishes and we make our way to the hotel to be locked away for the rest of the day. OK, so Christmas Day hasn't been what you might call conventional for a very long time and the solutions employed by players to compensate for not being at home, or having a few drinks while the Queen rabbits on about the Common-wealth, can sometimes wear a bit thin. But it's our Christmas and, while we may not necessarily like it this way, it's what we're used to.

Our Christmas starts in mid-December with the wholly inappro-priate but always memorable players' Christmas party. The planning that goes into arranging hotels, transport, a venue, entertainment, alcohol and, occasionally, women for 30 footballers, while also trying to get the money from each player to pay for it, shows a level of atten-tion to detail that is not always evident on the pitch.

The first time I attended one of these Christmas parties I wasn't sure what to expect. Fortunately, I wasn't quite the youngest player there, because that would have meant looking after the whip, which, as I recall, was £7,000 in cash from accumulated fines. That may not sound like a lot, but a five-figure sum would already have been used to hire the venue, staff and security, which equates to a lot of foreigners leaving their gloves on the training pitch (that's a fact, rather than a xenophobic attack). It is certainly a lot of money for an 18-year-old kid to look after, and it's a thankless task. It is essentially an evening lurching from one bollocking to another while being ruthlessly abused for either not being quick enough or messing up an order. When the whip runs out it is best to feign a life-threatening illness. Today that kid doesn't exist, which is a shame because it isn't easy watching young players having everything handed to them on a plate.

These Christmas parties can be impressive. We chartered a plane abroad on one occasion that ended in the hijacking of the plane's intercom, where a very funny player did impressions of managers past and present. As I recall, that Christmas party was in full fancy dress and started in the airport in England with a drinking game that involved the "Where's Wally?" character, ably played by one of our midfielders. Every half-hour or so Wally would intentionally go missing and the last person to realise and subsequently locate him would have to finish his drink. By the end of the night it seemed as if Wally was hiding all too frequently in the men's bathroom with his head in the toilet. At the same Christmas party, I remember a fight breaking out with a player from another team that was to do with a run-in earlier in the season. If you've always wondered who would win in a fight between Zorro and the Incredible Hulk, it's the Incredible Hulk every time.

A few Christmases ago, I was invited out by some friends who played for a team in the Championship. They had pulled all the stops out, which just meant that wherever we went we were penned in by two waist-height poles with a red rope running between them, a huge metal bowl full of ice and a magnum bottle of Grey Goose vodka, which seemed to be the fashion at the time. So long as you slipped the guy that ran the bathroom £20 and the guy that ran the floor £50, you would be well looked after with all the Paco Rabanne and girls that a man could ever wish for. I never take to the girls who are thrown into such pens. I don't know why – it's probably a combination of frustration and snobbery.

I told the player I was staying with that I was going to head back to his house and turn in. "You can't do that, you fucking clown," he objected. "What's my missus gonna say when you turn up and I'm still out?" He had a great point, albeit one that I had hoped he might not see after all the Grey Goose we'd downed. But these guys are very tuned in to these sorts of situations. A night out for them is like a work of art – get it right and you can drink all you want, have your ego massaged by fans and wannabe Wags and end up taking a young lady "up the west end", as we say in the trade. Get it wrong and you'll end up as another friend did – outside Panacea in Manchester with a bloody nose and no wallet.

At about 7am the lads finally ran out of places to go. The casino was closing, but not before one of the girls who worked there had taken one of my mates for about £5,000 in champagne and playing chips. (It wasn't until I saw her getting free drinks at the bar that I clocked what was going on, but when I told him he didn't care.) Our ringleader asked the girls where they were staying, and before long six of us – three guys and three girls – were crammed into a cab and on our way to a Holiday Inn just out of town.

If anything sums up this sort of girl better than the conversation that took place in that cab, I have yet to hear it. "So you play in the Championship? What's that – is it like the Premiership? Do you play against Wayne Rooney? Oh my God, you play lower down? Really? Oh my God, I can't believe I'm going to sleep with a Championship footballer." I don't know why I remember that cab ride so vividly but it has stuck with me ever since. I think it brought home to me the shift in mentality over the previous 10 years, which meant that some girls don't even know why they're sleeping with footballers any more. They don't even have the intelligence to ask why. It is almost as if they have been told that they should by subliminal advertising (otherwise known as red-top newspapers).

Once at the hotel, I tried to sleep in the lobby while a friendly porter brought me cups of coffee, probably out of pity. A couple of hours later the troops re-emerged from the lift. I try not to judge people on their looks (honestly), although we all do subconsciously, don't we? So I'll just say that when the chatty one from the cab reappeared in the lobby in her orange-peel Juicy Couture tracksuit it looked as if the night had caught up with her. This was not a girl I would take home to meet my mother. She gave my friend a kiss goodbye and then turned to me and said: "Imogen says to tell you you're a prick, by the way." (Imogen turned out to be one of the other two girls; her night had been cut short when I chose to stay downstairs in the lobby. She hadn't uttered a single word in my direction during the entire evening.)

I have come to enjoy Christmas parties, even if they will soon be a thing of the past, despite Manchester City's impressive attempts to fly the flag in their title-winning season. But there's no denying that there's less chance of trouble at our youth team's Christmas play, a low-budget but highly entertaining production featuring several of the first team's chief protagonists, the manager and his coaching staff. Everybody shifts in their seat in readiness for the ridiculing but by the end the whole room is in fits of laughter. The most recent was particularly good and, while not exactly worthy of any Oscar nominations, it did incorporate the chairman (usually the only exclusion), which probably put paid to a few first-year pro contracts.

Some would say that the only downside at this time of year is that there are so many games to play. Much is made of having a winter break. Yet the fixtures have to be played some time, and I don't see how players would be any fresher come the end of the season for two weeks off around Christmas, when, invariably, some would seize it as a chance to go on the lash.

Preparation is all-important at this time, with fitness a key component of any team's ambitions going into the Christmas run. For that reason some clubs keep the players in hotel rooms for as long as possible, even travelling from one away game straight to another and training on site. Not that this always works. I once stayed at a Manchester hotel where an office Christmas party was in full swing. I don't think I got any sleep that night, not least because a team-mate and his leggy accomplice evicted me from my room at 2am.

But it's not just at Christmas that fun can be had. Pre-season tours and mid-season trips can be a real cultural awakening, and not only on the pitch. On one occasion in Japan we stayed in a beautiful five-star hotel that, as luck would have it for some of the boys, was directly opposite an unassuming low-rise shack that turned out to be the local knocking shop. I was due to go along with the lads one afternoon but, suffering from jetlag, I passed out in my room, which was a shame because I'd have liked to further my research.

Stranger still was the time we spent in South Korea. We were given two nights out to explore the area and so we gave one of the hotel staff, a bellboy about 20 years of age, 200 Korean won (about £100) and agreed to buy his drinks all night. It was the smartest money anybody spent on that trip. He took us to the best places that Seoul had to offer and also filled us in on the etiquette, which at first we found quite bizarre, to say the least. In Seoul the best places are a combination of a restaurant, a bar, and private rooms all under the same roof. As you enter the building, the whole place opens up and if you look up all you can see are numbered doors with hundreds of porters running around on each floor, pulling groups of girls by their arms and literally throwing them into rooms that are occupied by groups of men.

The bellboy informed the head porter that we wanted to take a room and we duly took a lift to our level. The ferocity with which the girls were dragged and hurled into the rooms was a little hard on our western eyes. I have to say, I had assumed that all the girls were employees of the establishment but it turned out that they were locals having a night out. There were nurses, students, lawyers and teachers – this was their equivalent to a Saturday night at the Dog and Duck. Once in the room, we all took a seat around a huge table filled with every spirit imaginable. On one side of the room there was a flat-screen TV with karaoke, and in the corner there was a small bathroom. Ten seconds later the door flew open and three Korean girls were chucked in one after the other.

The bellboy explained how things worked. If a girl sits down, she is interested in getting to know you. If she sits down and immediately pours you a drink (always whisky), she already likes the look of you, and to reciprocate her advances you must down the whisky in one go. And there's more: if she offers to sing you a song on the karaoke machine, then your luck is well and truly in, but by the end of the song you must have put some money on the table to indicate that you would like to take her back to your place. The money isn't for the girl, but to show that you want to pay for a taxi. Got all that? I gravely offended three girls before I got the hang of it.

Before long each of us was sitting with a beautiful Korean girl; mine had been jet-propelled into the room and hurt her arm upon landing. Ever the gent, and because I was closest to the door, I picked her up and she came to sit down, pouring me a glass of whisky and introducing herself as Tory. I was wearing a hat that had a couple of badges (not as bad as it sounds) and she asked for one by pointing to it. Her English was non-existent and my Korean isn't exactly fluent. She kept telling me her name. We muddled on before she sang me a song but I kept my money in my pocket, much to the amusement of the other players. She sat back down beside me and gave me a frustrated look, and said again, "I'm Tory." I'm as polite as the next person but how many times can a girl tell you her name?

Just then, she turned to the bellboy and they had a chat in Korean before he leaned over to me and said: "You like her, yes?" I said: "Tell her she's very pretty." After a quick translation, she jumped up and sat on my lap. I immediately recognised this as a universal sign of affection rather than any etiquette exclusive to South Korea (I'm quick like that).

The guys around the table began to nudge each other and laugh; they knew how uncomfortable this sort of thing made me. I turned to the bellboy and asked him to tell Tory that I was flattered but enough was enough. He looked at me in confusion and spoke to her before turning to me and saying, "She's not called Tory."

"What's her name, then?"

"Sae Rin."

"So why has she been telling me her name is Tory all night?"

By this point the whole table was listening and everyone was just as confused as me. Sae Rin and the bellboy had another lightning exchange before the bellboy rolled over in fits of laughter. Sae Rin looked at me and buried her head under my chin to hide the fact that she was going a most extraordinary shade of crimson, despite having beautiful olive skin. The bellboy reappeared from under the table and, drying his eyes, explained: "She's not called Tory. She was telling you, 'I'm horny, I'm horny.'"

Eventually we parted on good terms. Claiming a breakdown in international communications, I retreated to the sanctuary of the hotel with my thoughts. I have never lived that incident down, and when I meet up with some of those old team-mates it isn't long before some smartarse brings it up. You can imagine how delighted that story makes my wife every time somebody re-tells it.

One of my regrets in football was saying to a hero of mine, "You look familiar – didn't you used to be somebody?" Hand on heart, it was meant as an ice-breaker (what are you supposed to say when you meet your hero?). But it backfired so spectacularly that our match was delayed as the officials and the stewards tried to restore order in the tunnel between the two sets of players.

In 2011-12, the behavioural standards in the Premier League appeared to hit a new low, in particular in relation to racism. John Terry, the former England captain, was cleared by a court of racially abusing Anton Ferdinand, but Luis Suárez received an eight-match ban after he was found guilty of the same offence following a row with Patrice Evra at Anfield.

Before I'm accused of passing judgment on others, let me make it clear that I am no saint on the football pitch – I've traded blows as well as insults. What I will say, though, is that I draw the line at racial abuse. My specialty has always been what cricketers call sledging and what footballers irritatingly refer to as banter. Over the years I have heard some fantastic acid drops that have cut players in half far more effectively than a crude tackle. Robbie Savage was a particular fan of what we in the trade call "cashing him off", which involves one player telling another how much money he has and how poor the other is in comparison. Not particularly classy but it seemed to work for Savage.

Occasionally, however, what starts out as harmless banter escalates into something physical. During one game I overheard an opponent tell my team-mate that he knew of somebody who had slept with his then-girlfriend, who was a famous singer. The remark went down badly, the mood of the game changed and every challenge thereafter seemed to end up with somebody in a heap on the ground. Only after the game, when we were breaking the two of them up in the away changing room, did the other players find out why the game had turned into such a battle. For the record, that rumour turned out to be true.

Much of what is said during matches is in jest. After all, there are a number of players who have been competing against each other for years, and because of that they have developed a relationship on the pitch, even though they don't know each other socially. There is a mutual respect, which helps to explain why, without realising, I collected several Manchester United shirts from the same player. If one of these players I've built up a rapport with was to foul me, then the chances are I'd let him help me up, knowing that he probably didn't mean to. Yet if another player I'd had a run-in with did the same thing, I would more than likely tell him where to go and ask the referee why he hadn't been booked. All of which, admittedly, does nothing to help relations.

Player behaviour isn't all down to the 11 who take to the pitch, however. I had a manager who used the physical side of the game as some kind of sadistic way to get a point across to an opposition manager that he didn't like. We always knew our manager had a bit of previous with his counterpart in the other dugout when we heard the words "This is a massive game" when it wasn't, or "We need to be physical on Saturday" when we didn't, or even "We owe them one", which simply meant he didn't like their manager. We'd nod our heads but never pay much attention to carrying out the instructions, because we felt we were better footballers than we were being given credit for.

Despite all this, it is the player and only the player who is in charge of his actions. There are mitigating circumstances, such as peer pressure and the dreaded red mist brought about by bad tackles and wicked comments, but the player must ultimately take responsibility for anything that he does on the pitch. I have watched myself back on TV a few times without recognising the individual who has lost all control; it happens, unfortunately. If only I had adopted the approach of a fellow professional who was having a great game against a very tricky team-mate of mine. As we jogged out for the second half, I asked what his secret was.

"We both know the same girl and I asked her along to watch today," he said.

"So what?" I replied naively.

"Well, she's sitting next to his wife."

CHAPTER 10
THE END LOOMS

I'm not sure if everyone I know is playing a practical joke on me, or whether, since I fell off my pedestal, people feel I'm not as bullet-proof as I once was. I raise the question because, for the last year or so, a succession of people, including friends, family, professional colleagues and those I have come to know in the media, have all felt brave enough to tell me that with the talent I have, or had, I should have played right at the top and for far longer.

I don't mind criticism, if indeed this is what it is, but at least tell me at the time rather than waiting until there is nothing I can do about it. I'm not saying I would have done something about it because, deep down, I'm not sure how much I really wanted to play at the very top, under the spotlight, once I became a footballer. There has always been something else calling me. I don't know what it is. In fact, I'm not sure it is any one thing in particular. It might simply be that I have convinced myself that life is too short to waste it playing football.

Towards the end of last season my agent rang. We usually talk for an hour or so every couple of weeks, on a variety of topics that include my favourites: if you could live anywhere in the world and do any job, where would it be and what would you do? (A hilltop villa in Ibiza, writing books while throwing good wine down my neck followed by loads of crusty bread and cured ham.) Where does the future of football lie? (A European superleague, without a doubt – it's just a question of when.) Why does he still work? (After years of talking to him, I am still no closer to finding out the answer.)

Eventually we'll turn to his specialist subjects, which include: how did the country get into this mess and what is the best way out? (Bad debt and greater exports.) What is happening at the club he supports? (Mismanagement, lack of funds.) How come I had more talent than the rest of his clients put together but didn't make the most of it?

It is a fair question but that doesn't make it any easier to answer. When anything comes to an end, there is a certain amount of grief involved that breaks down into five emotions, as any psychologist will tell you:

DENIAL AND ISOLATION

I played at the top level and earned tens of thousands of pounds a week. One of the clubs I played for made me their record transfer. I have won back-to-back player-of-the-year awards (I'll pause here to soak up the applause). I have won trophies and played against all the big-name players that the Premier League can offer. But sometimes a situation will develop where none of that counts for anything.

A few years ago, at the height of my earning power, I found myself in a position where all the good things I had going for me almost disappeared overnight at the hands of a manager on nothing more than an ego trip. After a Premier League match, the manager and I had a disagreement – the sort of exchange that happens in dressing rooms all over the country every weekend and which is normally quickly put to bed with a handshake. But in this case it led to the manager making an example of me in front of the whole squad.

From that moment on, I was marginalised to the extent that I was forced to change and train with the youth team, banned from talking to the media and even made to eat on my own, so that I had no contact with the first team. On the rare occasions that I would bump into a first-team player, even if it was in the car park first thing in the morning, I could see, as well as sense, how uncomfortable they felt being in my presence. Not because they disliked me; they were just scared shitless of being caught by the manager or one of his staff passing the time of day with a player who was made to feel like he had an incurable disease.

The hardest thing to take, among all of this ego-tripping, was that players whom I classed as friends – people whom I had sat next to on the coach for years and whom I had fought alongside in matches as if my life depended on it – were so worried about the same thing happening to them that they turned a blind eye to the disgraceful treat-ment of one of their own team-mates. In reality, though, I shouldn't have been surprised. On my first day as a professional I learned that everyone was in it for themselves.

ANGER

It annoys me that people feel they have the right to judge my career: pundits, fans, family and all. An American player I used to know was forever moaning about the mentality of "the British", as he put it. "If somebody does well for themselves over here," he'd say, "ya'll are jealous of them. In the States, folks are inspired by success." Historically, Americans and I have rarely seen eye to eye but on this point I do have to agree with him.

Nearly all the players I know feel that fans are jealous of the money they earn, the girls they attract and the lifestyle that some of them have. This is particularly clear when things are not going well on the pitch. I've been to a few fans' forums and the number of people who still shout, "I pay your wages" is amazing to me. It's the sort of argument a five-year-old would come out with. For years my stock reply was, "Well, surely you must live in a bigger house than me, then?" until I decided to find out from the club I played for how much of our wages was a direct reflection of ticket sales. The figure turned out to be around 26%, and the average for the Premier League is not much higher.

And another thing: I have studied football all my working life, and from the inside, so if you get into an argument with me about tactics, players, managers or whatever, I will know more than you, not the other way around. As my dad once said to me, it is OK to admit you are wrong. It infuriates me that people talk at me when they talk about football, and not with me. Football is such an emotive subject that everybody thinks their opinion is gospel. I don't need anyone to tell me how to play football; I know how to play football. I don't need anyone giving me a hard time; I expect everyone to be on my team all the time, even when things aren't going according to plan.

Years ago I was playing in a match when Rob Styles was the referee. I felt that he was favouring the bigger team (yet again) and told him so at every chance I got. Eventually there was a break in play and I made a point of having a strong word with him: "Fuck me, Rob, any danger of a decision here? It's a foul every time – you're fucking clueless." To which he replied: "Shut it! Have you ever refereed before?"

"No," I said. "Have you ever played football before?"

"Not as badly as you," he said.

I had to hand it to him – it was a great comeback and I have since used it a million times on referees in reverse. But he's still a prick.

BARGAINING

OK, I didn't win the World Cup, which was always my aim as a kid after my dad bought me that '86 Panini sticker album. But then not many players have; there are even fewer who are British. Relative to my talent, I think I did well. There are some places that I can visit where I'll never have to buy a drink, and there are some clubs where I'd probably be shot on sight by an angry mob – but that's about par for the course, surely? I never felt that I earned what I should have in relation to other players who seemed to have a PR machine behind them. On the other hand, I earned in a week what most of my friends earned in a year and I shared it with them as best as I possibly could.

I have lost count of the number of times I've taken my friends and family away on the annual holiday. I'm not bragging. In fact, it didn't start out that way at all. The way it evolved is, I think, far more interesting. In the beginning half a dozen of us would leave these shores for what can only be described as two weeks of very hard drinking, very hard flirting and, occasionally, very hard fighting brought on by the very hard drinking and flirting.

Then I began to earn more money than everyone else – put together. This led to new opportunities and inevitably my eyes were opened to a new culture and standard of living. Things became available as they never had been before. Fine wine, art, luxurious holiday destinations. Fine dining, large houses, new cars, expensive clothes. Women. I was exposed to a whole new world and a new culture. And I loved it. Most of the things I became interested in were simply due to my financial advisor diversifying my investment portfolio. I'm somebody who has never been able to buy a chocolate bar without knowing its life story, so it's easy to see how my interest was piqued. I'd go to galleries, wine tastings, great restaurants, all the time learning and soaking up influences, seeing what my class was missing out on.

Meanwhile, some of the lads began to meet the love of their life. In a move that I now realise was entirely selfish, I didn't like the thought of us not going away any more, so we began to go away together – family, friends, wives, kids etc. We have never, not once, had any problems, arguments or punch-ups, except when three or four of us threw a TV into a swimming pool shortly after England lost to Portugal in the quarter-finals of Euro 2004. But everyone makes mistakes. I know loads of people who have missed penalties.

Each year we seem to need a bigger villa to squeeze us all in, with our hired bikes, our hired cars and even our yoga instructors – requested by my dad, who has always told me to keep my feet on the ground. It's never been a problem, though. I pick up the bill for the villa and everyone else buys their flights and chips in for food and drink. We've pretty much covered the globe and plan to continue. It is, after all, one of life's rare pleasures to have everyone you love in such close proximity for a week or two without the stresses and headaches of day-to-day life. I know everyone else feels the same and is thankful to have seen and stayed in places that they never thought they'd have the chance to.

But some things I have tried to expose my friends to have not gone down as well as two weeks in the sun. One of my birthdays, for example, was without doubt an unmitigated disaster. The setting was a glamorous hotel, with a restaurant run by a very well-known chef...

We meet in London and it's raining – unfortunate but not exactly a surprise in Britain. Immediately I can see one or two of my friends are uncomfortable in a shirt and jacket, the restaurant's stipulated dress code. To them, a shirt and jacket would only be worn to a funeral and even then the deceased would have to be immediate family.

We enter the hotel. They're feeling very awkward now, out of their depth. I've been there – we've all been there – and it's not nice. I notice one of them has mud-encrusted laces. They haven't been undone since the shop assistant put the shoes in the box – they've been slipped on and slipped off hundreds of times and the heels are trodden down.

It's not a disaster but, equally, it's not good either. We're ushered in and shown to our table – rather hurriedly, it seems to me – and as we're taking our seats the sommelier wastes little time introducing himself. I order. Champagne to start, followed by a magnum of Château Mouton Rothschild from the year of my birth. The champagne doesn't touch the sides. What we have here is a simple case of mistaking a champagne glass for a shot glass and, despite the expectant glances in my direction, there is no more.

The food is served and the wine is poured. The food is cooked to perfection, of course; the wine is stunning. "Mate, where's the rest of it?" someone asks. Nine-tenths of the table laughs; the whole restaurant looks. The council estate kid in me finds it amusing but the new-found snob in me is outraged. "Yeah, bring the rest out, mate!" It's a lazy variation on the theme but still gets an overgenerous reception from our table. The resentment in the restaurant intensifies. Some of the waiters have heard. I step in. I explain that in a fine dining establishment things work a little differently – it's necessary to have a little more decorum and respect for the other diners. People pay a lot of money to be here and for some of them it may be the only time they come all year, or in the next five years, or ever, for that matter. The response is deafening: "HAPPY BIRTHDAY TO YOU, HAPPY BIRTHDAY TO YOU..."

I look over to the maître d': he's not happy and for a split second I'm on his side before I reaffirm my allegiance and tell myself that they (we) have as much right to be here as anyone else and that our money (my money) is as good as anyone else's. But there is no getting away from the obvious – we don't belong here, at least not as a group. I'm disappointed at myself, at them, at the staff, at everything. The disappointment quickly gives way to a cloudy anger; this is dangerous for me because it only comes on when I feel that I have been made to look stupid. The havoc that can result has become legendary within our group.

I pay the bill and am in two minds whether or not to leave a tip. I do, half out of guilt and half in case I ever go back or, indeed, any of the waiters recognise me and call the papers. It's happened before but not, I hasten to add, because of a light tip. Outside, I can't hold my anger in any more, launching into a full-scale attack and saying things like, "Was it too much to ask?" and, "Have you no shame?" Just as I'm really about to open up I notice the shoes, those muddy laces staring at me. They look sorry for themselves, ridiculous even. I feel terrible. It takes all the wind out of my sails and I stand there in the rain, looking and feeling pathetic. My best friend takes a few steps towards me and says that if I'm finished, I am more than welcome to join them in Yates's bar a couple of streets away. But I'll have to cheer up because I'm ruining my birthday for them.

In the pub the lads feel that, with a second round of Guinness imminent, enough time has passed to begin the jokes and offer up their true feelings without me taking offence. "That bloody red wine – how does anyone drink it? I hope it wasn't expensive." Everyone looks at me. "No, not really," I say. "I just thought it would go well with the food." In fact it cost £1,700 and I managed to squeeze out just over a glass, with most of the table leaving their fill.

At the end of the night a few of us decide to hail a cab and head back together. I'm staying with my parents and it's late. Eventually all but one of the bastards has been dropped off, a little worse for wear but on the whole much happier than at the outset. "Listen, mate," says my best friend, "I know it didn't go great but I've got to say that was the best pork I've ever tasted. Thanks for inviting me. Happy birthday." And with that he gives me a big kiss on the cheek, gets out of the cab and walks up to his door before turning to stick his thumb up and going inside.

I sit in the cab for a second, smiling to myself and staring at the council house he's just gone into, with its satellite dish dominating the weathered exterior and the rusting car in the garden. I admit that I miss this. Sometimes I really miss this. Perhaps we're not all cut out for the high life. Just because I revelled in it doesn't mean everyone will. Maybe they don't understand it. No. They don't want it, they don't need it, they're happy where they are... and who am I to force it on them or, in this case, down their throats? One thought, however, is uppermost in my mind as I see the TV flicker into life behind the faded orange curtains. "Fucking idiot," I mutter under my breath. "It was beef."

DEPRESSION

On Saturday, 26 November 2011, the Guardian published my column under the headline, "Sometimes there's darkness behind the limelight."

"The ability of football to turn life on its head with only a single blast of the referee's whistle makes it almost too easy to get carried away with the game at times," I wrote. "One minute everything is going well and seconds later things have never looked so bleak; sometimes that pressure is simply too much. Last week the attempt by the Bundesliga referee Babak Rafati to kill himself had pundits and commentators alike preferring to 'put football into perspective' rather than ask the awkward questions that nobody wants to answer.

"Many top sports people know only too well what Rafati is going through. On Friday, Stan Collymore, the former Liverpool striker, used his Twitter account to tell the world that his latest bout of depression was one of the most severe yet, prompting him to reveal that he hasn't seen daylight for four days. I certainly understand the feeling of wanting to shut yourself away from the world and when I was first diagnosed with depression in 2002 it was even more of a stigma than it is today.

"Since football exploded as a global business some 20 years ago the pressure on everybody involved has become a poisoned chalice. On the one hand the rewards are vast but on the other failure, or even mediocrity, can become the barometer against which all aspects of life are measured, albeit for a minority.

"Don't get me wrong: I am not saying for one minute that everyone involved with the game is in a state of irreparable depression, but I do think that the majority of us feel a degree of pressure, from the thought of what the headline writers have in store for us to the fans that start work on Monday morning unsure if they'll have enough money to put fuel in their car, never mind afford another £40 ticket come Saturday.

"When I started playing there was no media training or sports psychology to help you along the way; pressure was just something you had to deal with. Some players remain so anxious that they are physically sick before games, and one of my friends from the continent took to having oxygen, such was his fear of underperforming.

"On many occasions, I have seen players affected by what somebody has said about them on a message board or in a newspaper. Even if there are 99 positive comments, they will put all their efforts into searching for the one negative remark and, subsequently, put all their energy into worrying about it.

"A player, of course, knows only too well if he has played poorly, and yet the fear of seeing a below-par performance pulled apart by a journalist remains a huge obstacle for some. I must confess that in days gone by I have refused interviews with some reporters when I've felt that the rating out of 10 given to me in their match report the previous week did not reflect my true contribution. As I wrote that sentence I could see how pathetic it might sound but imagine having your performance in the workplace publicly graded every week.

"These examples of insecurity are in no way confined to the players. Whenever a manager mentions in an interview that he never reads the papers, then you know for certain that the first thing he does on a Monday morning is go through every match report with a highlighter pen.

"Adding pressure to your own game is sometimes unavoidable and can manifest itself in poor performances, the culmination of which can lead to a dark and depressing cul-de-sac. Tragically, there are examples of players who have reached this tipping point. In 2009 Robert Enke, the German goalkeeper, killed himself after struggling to come to terms with the death of his daughter, his illness not helped by an inability to deal with the scrutiny of his performances and anything less than his own high standards.

"Unfortunately, mental illness among the wealthy, and in particular those in sport that are perceived by the public to be doing the job they love, remains a tough concept for some to get their head around. The word 'depression' is suffering from a tired image and doesn't seem to have penetrated the public divide in perhaps the same way that, for example, post-traumatic stress disorder has.

"Yet, strangely for a game dominated by pent-up testosterone, the acknowledgment and treatment of depression is getting better.

Managers understand, perhaps more than ever, that the talent of a modern-day footballer will tend to put them in a position of wealth and fame at a very young age, bringing vulnerability as well as huge rewards.

"The media coverage of football has also changed, leading to a relentless quest for content that has driven an interest in the personal lives of many players. Because of this, I feel there is a real opportunity for our governing bodies to lay down a marker for what players can expect from the media and the terraces and what is an invasion of human rights.

"Some have asked why a banker, which Rafati is, would ever want to be a part of any of this. The added pressure of refereeing top-flight football is in evidence almost every day of the week but, while banking is certainly a way to make a good living, it is, first and foremost, a job. Football is a passion and in an ideal world something to live for, not to die as a result of.

"The world, of course, is far from ideal and that makes it easy for all of us to point the finger at times. Sometimes I'll see fans screaming at players of their own team with such anger that for a moment I lose all identification with them; the butterfly effect is the player that hurriedly makes his way to the coach as hundreds of kids wait for autographs.

"In my own way, I have learned to cope with the side-effects of this game but only because I believe, in fact I know, that if some of those involved with football have arrived at a moment in their lives where they feel that standing in front of a train or slitting their wrists in a hotel room is the only way out, then it isn't just a game any more, is it?"

I submitted this column very early in the week because the subject was so sensitive. As I recall, there were many phone calls back and forth to the Guardian with questions like: was I sure I wanted this to go to print? Who else besides the club doctor knew about my depression? Was I prepared for the comments that would inevitably follow, because there would be some people who would not be sympathetic to a footballer suffering from depression? After careful consideration I made a last-minute decision to go ahead. The subject was too important and I wanted the readers to know that professional football isn't all champagne and skittles. Sometimes, as the sub-editor put it with his headline, there is indeed a darkness behind the limelight. The column went in completely untouched save for one detail: the editor came back to say that where Babak Rafati was concerned, I couldn't write, "commit suicide" as this term is deemed offensive and upsetting for the families. Instead, I had to write "kill himself". And, no, I can't see the difference either.

I'd expected a barrage of comments questioning how I could be depressed, but the feedback was overwhelmingly positive. Nothing, however, could have prepared me or anyone else in football for what happened the following day. I remember getting a phone call, asking if I had seen what was scrolling on the bottom of one of the sports channels. I turned on and saw the words, "Wales manager Gary Speed found dead at his home." I remember having a horrible thought when I first saw the news (and before I am accused of being even more vain and self-centred than I actually am, I can only tell you the truth about what my first instinct was): I wonder if he'd read the column.

The problem with today's world of instant communication is that rather than taking the time to work out if what they are about to type, text or tweet is helpful or considered, many people do it anyway and ask questions later or, in some cases, never. Virtually every text in my inbox read in a similar vein: "Gary Speed has hanged himself... Do you think he read your column?"

The fact that all of us were on the same wavelength that day was anything but comforting. It was nothing more than a horrendous coincidence, but the sentiment of that column was, to some degree, played out in real time and in real life that very morning, and it was horribly unsettling. Whatever the truth is about Speed's death (and I have no desire to find out) it was a tragic example of the pressures that some people, for whatever reason, keep locked away inside.

I didn't know Speed personally but I know many people who did. I've played against him and teams that he's managed and nobody had a bad word to say about him, save for a few sentences reserved for the way he bowed out, leaving his family behind. I had a heated argument with another player that afternoon, after he labelled everyone who kills themselves a coward. That argument is something that I find quite offensive because it makes a lot of assumptions based on no foundations whatsoever.

Whatever the reason behind Speed's death, it shows us that nobody, no matter how successful or well liked, is immune from the torment that the mind can conjure up. And I can share in some of that because, although I'm only a footballer, a certain amount of my life has been spent in the shadow of what came to be known as the "dark forces", with football as the chief protagonist. Football can go one of two ways: either you embrace every part of it and it becomes your life; or, and this is the case where I am concerned, you rebel against certain parts of it but they never go away and you end up continually shovelling shit against the tide before eventually being consumed by hate, guilt, anger and bitterness.

Depression had always been there but it took football at the highest level to really bring it to the fore. Where once I could ignore the catcalls from the stands, I suddenly hit the point where I didn't want to take that abuse any more and I'd answer back. I never smiled for pictures with fans, I didn't train if I didn't want to and I didn't bother to make small talk with other players who I didn't have anything in common with. I drank more and I argued with the manager (more than normal).

At its worst I was reclusive and extremely volatile in situations that required me to conform, such as sponsored events. Although nearly everyone I came into contact with simply thought that I was an arrogant prick, the club doctor suspected otherwise and called me into his office. "How is your mental health?" he asked. I didn't know it at the time, but the doc specialised in mental health. No sooner had he told me than I made the decision to confide in him everything that had been happening for the last 10 years – the history, the previous diagnosis, the short temper, everything.

Initially the doc focused on the misdiagnosis of "manic depression" as it was then, now known as bipolar disorder. There are many forms of the illness but the long and short of it is that the sufferer goes through huge lulls in their life where the slightest menial task is impossible until eventually they enter into complete withdrawal.

This period is followed by a huge burst of energy that manifests itself in what "normal" people would call irrational, eccentric or just plain crazy behaviour.

Following a big-money move that went spectacularly wrong, I found myself cast adrift with the rest of the "bomb squad" – the football equivalent of the yellow group at primary school. This essentially meant that, barring a horrific coach accident on the way back from an away game, I was never going to play for the club again. Even if that did happen, it would still be touch and go.

Living so far away from my family meant that I had plenty of time to let my mind take over, which has always proven to be dangerous. Late one night a friend and I had one too many of something or other, which led to a succession of ideas being floated in an attempt to relieve the monotony of a career that was going nowhere. The one idea that stuck was definitely the most risky, certainly the most stupid and without doubt the best by a country mile.

Wednesdays are traditionally a footballer's day off. In a normal week, Monday will be an easy day after Saturday's match, Tuesday is a bit more up-tempo and Thursday and Friday are more technical and tactical days as the manager prepares the formation and strategy ahead of the challenge of the weekend.

Training at this point for me was mind-numbing. My understanding is that there are supposed to be a certain number of professionals to put on a training session, yet very often at this time our sessions had about four people. Nobody ever complained because nobody wanted to listen. The players didn't want to be there and nor did the coach and so, as long as those who were present kept it to themselves, the coach was happy to knock it on the head after an hour or so. It also helped enormously that I was rooming with the guy taking the session.

Sitting in our two-bed flat, we made a list of all the major destinations that we could fly to and from in a day. The bulk of them were obviously in Europe but there were also one or two in north Africa. It started off innocuously enough. Every Wednesday we turned up at the airport and picked a place that we knew we could visit without too much drama. But by the end it had spiralled completely out of control. Leaving the country, without permission, while the season is going on, regardless of whether you are playing or not, carries at least a two-week fine. Given my standing at the club, I would probably have been sacked as well.

The second incarnation of "fight or flight" involved finding out which flights were on and picking a random destination out of a saucepan that was otherwise reserved for the pasta that we'd been eating every night for a year. Once there we'd have to do whatever the other demanded and, as a result, I have proposed to four women in my life: a Swedish girl called Anna, a French girl called Yvette, a Czech girl called Markita, and my wife, with a satisfactory 50% success rate. In fairness, though, Yvette would probably have married anyone.

Other highlights included bungee-jumping, hitch-hiking to a tiny suburb of Tirana called Kamëz with two guys, both of whom I am sure were in the mafia, flying to Brno dressed as Batman and Robin, donning our best suits and pretending to be incompetent doormen outside the Four Seasons in Paris until we were eventually outed by one of the hotel's regular customers, and so much that is illegal that I won't even write it anonymously. But it wasn't manic depression or bipolar or whatever anybody wants to call it that brought this on. It was pure rebellion, brought about by boredom and frustration (that's a self-diagnosis, by the way, rather than the two misdiagnoses of bipolar).

I don't want sympathy and I've never asked for it. After all, it took me 10 years to ask for help. But I will say that, at its worst, depression is a most horrible illness. It can make the sufferer appear as if he is arrogant, rude, lazy and introverted, and that is on a good day.

In my house I had an Eames chair. It wasn't very comfortable but it looked the part. More importantly, it was the first chair I saw when I came home from training. During the worst days of the dark forces, I'd walk through the door, sit down in this chair and there I would stay until bed. Many sufferers of depression talk of a place that is like a magnet for them, a place where they feel safe and where they do not have to see anyone or do anything. The Eames chair was a place of safety for me and most definitely a magnet. I sat in that chair because I knew that once I did, I would not have to get up again to do something that I couldn't face.

Everybody knew that once I'd sat down in that chair I would not be moving. My wife knew this: she would catch me on the way in at the front door, turn me around and take me into town for lunch or to help her run an errand. I spent the whole time looking at my mobile phone (I don't own a watch), wishing that the seconds would go faster so that I could get back to my chair. Once in the chair, that was it for the rest of the day. It almost felt like a form of paralysis: I simply could not get up. It was as if there was an invisible weight on my lap preventing me from doing anything. I should point out that the TV wasn't on, I didn't have a book, I didn't talk: I just sat there, hour after hour, day after day, dreading going to bed because I knew that the next time I opened my eyes, I'd have to leave the house for training and it would all start again.

Today, aided by 15mg of Mirtazapine, which acts as an anti-depressant sleeping pill (an oxymoron if ever there was one), and 20mg of Citalopram every morning (it was 40mg but I suffered from terrible lockjaw, caused by an ingredient similar to the MDMA in the ecstasy pills that I first encountered as a 17-year-old), I am a completely different person. I still have bad days but I don't wake up dreading the day ahead, I don't look out of the training ground window wishing I could be as far away as possible and I don't look at every single task as if it were the equivalent of climbing Everest. No amount of pill-popping can make standing in line at the bank or pushing a trolley around Tesco an enjoyable experience but at least I can do those small things now.

For a time my football improved beyond any reasonable expectation that I had. It felt as if somebody had given me back 20/20 vision. I know that sounds strange but when you're in the middle of something like depression, autopilot becomes your best friend. Part of the brain takes over everything and, cruelly, does the bare minimum to get you through. I'd like to say that sitting down with somebody was the key to my recovery but that would be bullshit: it was the drugs and in particular the dose of Citalopram that helped.

When the club doctor prescribed them to me, he said: "I have had a lot of success with these... Oh, and you can't overdose on them either, before you get any ideas." He wasn't the only one who felt the need to be cautious. Initially I was referred to a London clinic (for the record I did not want to go) and after two hours with a young man who simply sat and said, "I see" and, "How does that make you feel?" I concluded that I was wasting my time. At the end of the session he said, "I'm going to be honest with you. I am concerned for your safety and I would feel more comfortable if you had somebody who could escort you home." He was so concerned that his office never rang back to book me in for a second appointment. I wonder if he wonders what became of me.

Therapy is a very odd experience. I sat for hours on end while strangers asked me: "When was the last time you were violent? When did you last think about killing yourself? In that vision, how did you kill yourself?" I thought it all sounded suspiciously like something from Pink Floyd's The Dark Side of the Moon, and so I'd answer: "I am not frightened of dying. Any time will do, I don't mind. Why should I be afraid of dying? There's no reason for it, you've got to go some time," which as Floyd fans will know are lines from the album. They never twigged. But much of the material for my column came from this time, which leads me to suspect that there may be something in the manic depression diagnosis. For example, my iTunes "most listened to" tracks were a remnant of a (hopefully) long-gone incarnation of myself. At the top was Love Will Tear Us Apart by Joy Division, whose lead singer, Ian Curtis, killed himself and whose lyrics such as "When routine bites hard and ambitions are low" played on my mind for years. I tried to shoehorn them into nearly every column, without success.

Second was Peter Gabriel's We Do What We're Told (Milgram's 37), a song about the controversial experiments carried out by the social psychologist Stanley Milgram. The song includes distant tortured screaming, which I used to appreciate very much, and this

I did manage to get into a column. Third was Bob Dylan's stunning It's Alright Ma (I'm Only Bleeding), which is a song that still drives me to distraction. The poetry is so good that any attempt to get near it is simply a waste of time. It has one line, in particular, that completely flipped me out for a while: "While preachers preach of evil fates, teachers teach that knowledge waits, can lead to hundred-dollar plates, goodness hides behind its gates, but even the president of the United States sometimes must have to stand naked."

I remember being very apprehensive about succumbing to pills. In an ideal world, it would be nice to think that a person could return to a healthy mental state naturally rather than relying on chemicals, especially as there is already a lot of other help out there. Cognitive behavioural therapy, or CBT if you're really lazy, involves working with an expert to essentially rewire how the brain has come to perceive the outside world and everyday situations. In my case, I had gone for years piling up negative thoughts and honing a self-deprecating attitude towards everything in my life that was good, especially football. CBT reboots that mindset while allowing you to confront all the things that the brain has parked that it didn't want to deal with, essentially wiping the slate clean. Of course it is difficult to tell how much of my new-found outlook is thanks to the CBT rather than the drugs. For fear of not wanting to confront the thought that I have spunked £300 a week for the last year on CBT classes, I will go on record as saying that it is probably 50/50, and now I consider that matter well and truly parked.

For the record, I never thought I'd be this old. My career has flown by; there have been unbelievable highs and terrible lows that I will never get over. When I was a kid, my dad told me the story of one of his heroes, Peter Green, from the original Fleetwood Mac. Desperate to keep up the group's initial success, Green's bandmates began to exert pressure on him to turn out another hit. In the mid-70s Green underwent electroconvulsive therapy in a psychiatric hospital after being diagnosed with schizophrenia, brought about by his failure to accept the fame and success of the band that he had founded. He had even grown his fingernails to the point where he could no longer play the guitar. I only remembered that story a few paragraphs ago – probably because, as I sit here, typing out the last few pages of this book, I know that, if I'm honest with myself, for about a year I have been drinking very heavily and eating excessively in a pathetic attempt to develop a gut so that they won't pick me any more. The last thing that I want to do is play football again. I don't want to go back. Don't make me go back.

ACCEPTANCE

OK, hands up. I never reached my potential. I have too many character flaws that prevent me from performing consistently in almost anything that I do. Everything else is just an excuse. But football is a cruel game. It doesn't even itself out as the pundits would have us believe, because there are teams that are incredibly talented and teams whose players need to make up for their lack of talent by running farther and kicking harder. On a personal note, I am at fault for taking too much interest in things that were going on away from the pitch, and my career suffered as a result. The higher a player goes in football, the more there is to take into account, and if you can't manage it all correctly – which I didn't – it may just be your undoing.

Image rights contracts are a prime example, and they are certainly worth having providing you don't abuse the system. Much has been written about these contracts and yet not much is understood. Let's start at the beginning.

If a football club recognise that they will benefit from exploiting your image, which essentially is the most personal intellectual property that a person has, then that recognition needs to be reflected financially. In other words, they should pay the player for it through an agreement in his contract.

Here's how the system works in music. If I have a photograph of Paul McCartney or Liam Gallagher that is worth a lot of money and I want to exploit it commercially, I would have to strike a deal with the record label that owns the commercial rights to the artist. If the record label feels that I am offering enough money and it, in turn, can pay its artists a healthy cut to make it worth their while, then I could in theory exploit the image.

It's similar in football. If a company or partner of the football club wishes to exploit the image or name of a particular player, then remuneration must be made to the club. Where football differs slightly is that the remuneration to the player is pre-set and, generally, does not work on a pay-as-you-go basis. To clear one thing up, image rights contracts are not illegal, but they are shrouded in an incredibly murky shade of grey. If any image rights contract were ever to go to court, then there would be plenty of convincing arguments on both sides.

When image rights contracts first caught on, lots of agents began to insist that clubs paid their players through companies that had been set up purely to avoid tax. That's not to say that the players didn't have an image that was worth exploiting: every player could make a good case for a certain percentage of their wages or signing-on fees to be paid through an image rights company, because nearly every player has had his name put on a club shirt and sold through the club shop. The grey area concerns the exact figure that a player should receive from the club for his image rights because – and I don't know for sure – Wayne Rooney, for example, probably outsells Dimitar Berbatov in the club shop.

David Beckham would be easy to make a case for. His image and name are worth millions of pounds because they help to sell a vast array of products in the club shop and elsewhere around the globe. The bargaining position that Beckham finds himself in is that LA Galaxy can pay him a huge salary because they sell so much Beckham-branded merchandise. Essentially this "wage' isn't for playing football – it is simply an advance on branded goods that the club and its partners sell across the length of his contract.

This type of contract is one of the few that has to be paid in monthly instalments as money is recouped because the figures are so high. Rather than being paid directly to Beckham, the salary will be paid to a company that has been set up specifically to manage Beckham's image rights. This company then pays out a dividend to its shareholders at the end of the financial year. These shareholders usually number one person in total: the player. The "loophole", as the media like to call it, is that any tax due will be paid at the corporation rate rather than the far higher personal rate.

Nobody could argue that Beckham's image isn't worth millions of pounds but there are many abuses of this tax loophole. I heard of two players at one of the top Premier League clubs who were being paid up to 75% of their weekly wage through companies set up to manage their image rights. Clearly, that is a massive piss-take and the taxman does not take kindly to having his face rubbed in it.

When I started playing football I had nothing. Ever the romantic, I used the last £5 to my name to buy my girlfriend and myself some fudge and a can of Coke each on Blackpool pier. Shortly after that, I signed my first professional contract for £500 a week – a lot of money given where I had come from. I went on, with the aid of an image rights company, to earn tens of thousands of pounds a week. I like to have money but only because I like to invest it and help my family and friends. I have never been cash-rich because every penny has been invested. Some of that money will be lost when the "new Facebook" that I had high hopes for turns out to be the new Myspace. Conversely, some of that money will perhaps be returned to me with a healthy profit on top, certainly if the other companies that I have invested in continue to turn over money at the rate that they currently are. But the problem with living to your means is that you very rarely have any cash left for emergencies.

And when Her Majesty's Revenue & Customs finally decides that it has had enough of football and its multimillionaire players with their tax loopholes, clever agents, image rights companies and army of accountants, well, that's when the whole shithouse can go up in flames. As I have found out. All the Revenue has to do is send out a tax bill big enough to make contesting it too expensive to contemplate, because what if you lose? The scary thing is that my bill was one of the smaller ones. I have heard that there are players at almost every Premier League club who have been hit with a similar bill and are paying up just for a quiet life and to spare themselves any public embarrassment. I heard on the grapevine about one Midlands player who has been told to cough up not far off £5m.

During the boom years of the Premier League, these problems could not have seemed further away. We had a beautiful detached house with five bedrooms, a games room, a cinema and so many other rooms that I don't think I ever went in all of them. I had a full-sized snooker table that was used at the World Championships, as well as a collection of games consoles that sat on a £6,000 custom-made sideboard where they simply gathered dust. Our furniture was all imported from Italy and certain pieces housed a large collection of the most sought-after and highly revered vintages of the last 30 years, from Bordeaux and Burgundy.

The house had its own mini-spa, including a hot tub, sauna and twin bath with a built-in TV that sat in its own wet room. Every wall in the house displayed a piece of art, the star of which was an etching by Picasso bought at auction through Bonhams. I had a network of dealers who would call me well before the most desirable pieces made it anywhere near the saleroom.

I had bespoke suits made on Savile Row and my wife had a bespoke wedding dress. Her rings came from the private room at Tiffany's on Bond Street, as did her necklaces and earrings. I drove the kids to their £3,000-a-term private school in one of three brand new cars, one of which was an imported limited edition.

We holidayed in Barbados and Dubai and rented villas costing up to £30,000 a week that came with their own butlers and staff. In a really flush year, I'd fly my family and friends out to join us on private jets that were stuffed with champagne and the finest spirits. I hired chefs to cook three meals a day for 30 guests and booked VIP tables at the trendiest nightspots. When we'd have a party at the house, I'd book DJs and bands to play for us. We had memberships to all the top hangouts across London (not that we went to many of them) and mixed with the rich and famous over dinner and at charity nights in five-star hotels.

Today, most of that has gone. The tax bill that I received has all but wiped me out and everything that football bought me has been sold off. Well, not quite everything. A few months ago, I was having one last clear-out of the cupboards in the unused rooms of the house. If truth be told, I was looking for things to sell. At the back of one of these rooms there is a shower room. The shower screen door still had a sticker from the company that custom-made it to the shape of the room, together with that blue see-through film that gives so much satisfaction when you peel it away from the glass. Thick dust had stained the bottom of the white wall where it had been collecting for two years. Underneath the sink were some beautifully made Italian towel drawers that had never actually seen a towel, or an Italian, but were beautiful nonetheless. I'm not sure if it was desperation or curiosity that made me open the bottom drawer, the bigger of the two, because to the best of my knowledge nobody had been anywhere near them since the fitters put them in.

The click of the drawer echoed in the room as it slid open and the motion kicked up a layer of dust that had settled underneath. It felt thick and heavy as it settled back down over my face and arms. Inside, I could see a large crinkly blue bag with blue handles; each one had the familiar line of yellow writing that said IKEA. As far as I knew we didn't have anything in the house that had come from IKEA. But the bag was full – the weight of the drawer had told me that, even though I had never opened it before. It was bulging around the sides too, so whatever was in there couldn't be the conventional IKEA staples such as a toilet roll holder, a set of knives and forks, a picture frame that doesn't match anything, and that odd glass to replace the one that smashed nine years ago at your first house and that your wife, with her freakish elephant-like memory, refuses to let go of. Anyway...

Confused, I slowly pulled the handles apart. There was a faint mustiness that only confused me further. "Why have we got a load of red bedding down here?" I wondered. We'd never had red bedding at any of our houses and nor, I like to think, would we. Furthermore, we have never had silk sheets – even when the money was raining down on us, there were some things that I could never be convinced about. As I reached in I saw that, whatever this was, it was quite small, with only a single fold from left to right. It certainly wasn't a duvet cover – it must have been a rogue pillowcase purchased in a moment of extreme panic, probably after an unwelcome relative invited themselves to stay. But as I pulled at the fold, white writing began to appear: first an A and then an L. I kept pulling until I could see the whole word written on this red fabric. It read ALONSO.

That IKEA bag went on to give up a veritable Who's Who of Premier League players past and present, and I spent the best part of an hour in that empty room pulling out shirt after shirt. On the heels of Alonso came Keane, who was soon joined by Fábregas and Adebayor. Then Johnson and Doyle, together with Lescott, Rodwell and Hyypia. It didn't stop there: the bag produced the Championship-winning shirts of Ferdinand and Vidic (the highly collectable ones with the golden Premier League badges on the arms). There were the shirts of Cahill, Davies, Woodgate and Richards. I found more belonging to Cuéllar, Parnaby, Carlisle, Bale, Onuoha, Keane (the other R Keane), Huddlestone and Berbatov, as well as dozens of others. I even had a Leeds United home shirt, signed by the entire squad after their run to the semi-finals of the Champions League. All told, there must have been 60 shirts jammed into the bag.

For somebody who knows the value of Premier League shirts, this was a moment of divine intervention. I estimated that there had to be at least £30,000-40,000 worth of shirts, not taking into account the premium that one could expect for the top players. On a good day in the auction room, and with a strong following wind, those shirts might easily see their way past the £50,000 mark. Feeling more than a little smug I retired to bed and slept soundly for the first time in nearly six months.

The next morning I woke up with a new determination. The shirts had provided a lifeline and I knew it. I spent the rest of that day making phone call after phone call in an attempt to find the right homes for them. As the afternoon became the evening I eventually finished making my calls, tired, emotional and extremely happy. I had been given a second chance to prove myself after more than a dozen years of playing professional football. I had a golden opportunity to put a stop to all the madness and the bullshit and I wasn't going to mess it up again.

Today, nearly all those shirts can be found framed in the homes of everybody that I hold dear to me. My friends were only too happy to be the beneficiaries and they make a point of showing them off to me whenever I drop in for a catch-up. I never get tired of seeing how proud they are to have them hanging on their wall. It does, as Phil Daniels once sang, give me a sense of enormous well-being.

The cull of my football career didn't stop at the shirts. I found new homes for all the signed programmes that various kit men had collected for me down the years. I gave away all the signed prints that I never looked at and which had been consigned to a shoebox somewhere in the depths of my triple garage, and the balls that I'd accumulated from important games. In the back garden, we had a bonfire and set light to every newspaper clipping that I had ever collected. I gave away all my player-of-the year awards, my player-of-the-month awards and every bottle of man-of-the-match champagne that I'd received over the seasons. There were 57 of them in total. But who's counting? I also gave away my medals. Every one of them.

I desperately needed that £50,000 but that isn't the point. The shirts, the signed prints, the medals and the individual awards all went towards making the people that I love extremely happy. And, more importantly – where my own wellbeing is concerned, anyway – I have finally turned the last page of a very turbulent chapter of my life. Materially I may be worse off, financially I may be some way short of my peers, but where contentedness is concerned, every one of them looks up to me. My football career, colourful and unique as it has been, will always be there to see for anybody who has nothing better to do. My name is in the history books; it is on hundreds of thousands if not millions of web pages; and, in some places, it is even chipped in stone. But more important than any of that rubbish is the fact that my name will live on in real life and in real time, through my children. And that, as I continually remind myself, is the one thing that the bastards can never take away from me.

INDEX

(the initials SF in subentries refer to the Secret Footballer)

Gullit's slating of and
 encounter with 192–3
"honorary brother" labelling
 of 12
house of, described 216–17
investments of 216
lockjaw suffered by 209
man-of-the-match awards won
 by 11
manager's window smashed
 by 12
Manchester United shirts
 collected by 186
and *Match of the Day* 109, 110
"mercenary" accusation
 against 58
and methadone 57–8
newspaper cuttings burned by
 221
non-league career of 8–9
101 Great Goals practised by
 4–5
parents encourage football
 career of 6
parents of, *see* father; mother
player-of-the-year awards won
 by 192
police escort for 14
Savile Row suits of 217
secret trips of 207–8
signed programmes disposed
 of by 220–1
signing of 9, 10
Sky's punditry-role approach
 to 73
"street football" preferred by 3
and tabloid journalists 57; *see
 also* media
tax bill sent to 216, 218

in therapy 210–11, 212
training becomes mind-
 numbing to 207
transfer of 86, 99–100, 192,
 206
Twitter followers of 119–39
virtual nobody status of 14
warned off media 64, 69
women proposed to by 208
work experience of 64
"Secret Footballer" column 68
 inspiration for 5–6
sexuality 46–9
Shakespeare, William 6
Shevchenko, Andriy 81, 152
Silva, David 156
Sinclair, Trevor 111
"six degrees of separation" 39
Skrtel, Martin 92
Sky TV 64, 73, 127
 Neville on 80
 24-hour sports channel of 71
Smalling, Chris 87–8
Soccer AM 73
Soccernomics 84–5, 86, 88
Sócrates 5
Speed, Gary 204
sponsorship 28–9, 71, 112
statistics 82–6, 88
Stoke City FC 86, 88, 104
"street football" 3
Styles, Rob 194
Suárez, Luis 39, 41–2, 46, 85, 185
 fans' taunting of 41
Sweden national side 81

tackling 90–2, 107–8
 see also tactics
tactics 77–92

229